D0458186

Date Due

MADAME
AMBASSADOR

Bilingual Press/Editorial Bilingüe

General Editor
  Gary D. Keller

Managing Editor
  Karen S. Van Hooft

Associate Editors
  Barbara H. Firoozye
  Thea S. Kuticka

Assistant Editor
  Linda St. George Thurston

Editorial Board
  Juan Goytisolo
  Francisco Jiménez
  Mario Vargas Llosa

Address:
  Bilingual Press
  Hispanic Research Center
  Arizona State University
  P.O. Box 872702
  Tempe, Arizona 85287-2702
  (480) 965-3867

MADAME AMBASSADOR

The Shoemaker's Daughter

Mari-Luci Jaramillo

Bilingual Press/Editorial Bilingüe

Tempe, Arizona

ISBN 1-931010-04-8

Library of Congress Cataloging-in-Publication Data

Jaramillo, Mari-Luci.
  Madame Ambassador, the shoemaker's daughter / Mari-Luci Jaramillo.
    p. cm.
  ISBN 1-931010-04-8 (alk. paper)
    1. Jaramillo, Mari-Luci. 2. Women ambassadors—United States—Biography. 3. Ambassadors—United States—Biography. 4. Women civil rights workers—United States—Biography. 5. Mexican American women—Biography. 6. Honduras—Foreign relations—United States. 7. United States—Foreign relations—Honduras. I. Title.

E840.8.J38 A3 2001
327.73'0092—dc21
  [B]   2001023126

PRINTED IN THE UNITED STATES OF AMERICA

Cover and interior design by John Wincek, Aerocraft Charter Art Service

Acknowledgments

Partial funding provided by the Arizona Commission on the Arts through appropriations from the Arizona State Legislature and grants from the National Endowment for the Arts.

*To all who took a moment
to make a difference
in my life*

$\mathcal{C}$ ontents

Preface

There were days when I thought I would never finish this book. My purpose in writing it was to send a personal message to the reader, so that initial desire made me continue.

Foremost, I wanted students to read it. I wanted the message to be that they can achieve. To do this, they must stay in school, work hard and achieve their goals. It takes perseverance, hard work, and persistence. Students should realize that no matter what cards they are handed, they can overcome. My words of advice are to focus, focus, focus and don't ever give into the temptation of abandoning school.

I also wanted to reach a second group, mainly those who have struggled with poverty and discrimination, albeit subtle at times, but who have surpassed all these obstacles and received an education and are now enjoying a measure of success. By conquering their trials and tribulations, they can now say, "We did it." They achieved what seemed impossible. They should be proud of their accomplishments and of who they are—fine role models for students.

Another group I hoped would be inspired are those who are in a position to influence the young: teachers, parents, mentors. In my own case, I had always been surrounded by people who encouraged me to excel. Later on there were those who offered advice, provided moral and financial support, and helped in numerous other ways. Like my mentors, all of you have the potential to be the deciding factor in a student's life so that he or she can succeed. There is a student out there who needs encouragement and a person who will believe in him or her. Please locate that student and offer your help and support. *Gracias.*

Acknowledgments

During my tour of duty as ambassador to Honduras, there was not a day that went by without some kind of humorous adventure taking place. These stories were such that I felt they should be shared and thus began my first attempt at writing a book.

After my assignment ended in Honduras, I took back with me to the States 450 pages of stories that I thought would become my book. But during the last six or seven years of my career, I realized that no longer were the entertaining events the most important thing I needed to share. My entire story from my earliest memories to the present replaced the earlier fun-filled pages. Not only did I want to share with the world some of my wonderful personal and professional experiences, but it seemed imperative to send a clear message to the young people who still had their life's journey ahead of them. Maybe I could help them overcome some of the barriers they are sure to face.

But it was very difficult to decide what to include in such a book. Should I emphasize the professional side or my personal life? Many friends advised me to describe both aspects in great detail. I decided to follow their advice and you are about to read the results of their suggestions and my desires.

There are many people who helped me along the way not only to start writing, but also to shape this book. The initial person outside my immediate family who really became interested in my task and helped me all the way through was a close friend, Dr. Ronald Blood. He encouraged me almost daily. He motivated me when I was letting go of my dream. At the time, I didn't even know if I would continue. The task seemed monumental and overwhelming.

Writing a book was a brand new experience for me. Something had happened to the enthusiasm with which I had first started. I was extremely busy when I retired; I was building an addition to my house and getting used to the idea of not having a job. And for many months, my travels still continued at breakneck speed. Somehow the new effort that was composed of only two chapters fell off the front burner and I had just about given up.

About a year after I had made the initial start, two other people motivated me and offered me physical help to get going. Dr. Ricardo Dow y Anaya and his wife, Joy, offered to help type my rough notes. After getting through the initial messy handwritten notes, they suggested I could dictate and Joy transcribe. I dictated, Joy transcribed, Ron edited, and Ricardo cheered.

I am forever grateful to those whom I have mentioned, as well as those that I have received assistance from in various forms during the development of this book.

Thank you all. *Mil gracias a todos.*

Senate Confirmation Hearing

Once again, feeling like the timid and reserved shoemaker's daughter of my childhood, I shook my head in awe at the huge, beautiful, richly paneled room in the Rayburn Building in the middle of Washington, D.C., How on earth had I gotten from my small hometown in northern New Mexico that still bore signs of its original Spanish settlers, to this elegant Senate hearing room? For some reason, that room with its feeling of hushed anticipation of something exciting about to happen, seemed very familiar to me. I certainly thought that I had been there before, although I knew I had only walked in the corridor as a tourist. It was probably imprinted on my mind because of my passion for TV news and politics. The richly colored mahogany desk at the front of the room appeared to be sitting on a dais of sorts, with an extension around the top that served to hide the hands, paper, and other articles belonging to the people sitting there. The senators and staff seemed very familiar also. But even more noticeable was the long table and its three or four chairs directly in front of that gigantic, intimidating desk. Having observed hundreds of television newscasts, testimonies, or interrogations that could sometimes be serious and thought-provoking, I was intimidated, wondering what my hearing would be like today. I repeated the silent prayers my grandmother had taught me in my youth over and over, calling on my favorite saints to assist me and give me the courage to survive the next few minutes.

As I concentrated on remembering to breathe, I looked around at the rest of the very grand room. It was filled with wooden chairs featuring smart wine-colored leather upholstery, all facing toward the front of the room. Reporters, observers, and other visitors usually sat in this section. It too was often panned by the television crews, but today the large historical room was almost vacant. There was nothing significant, as far as the reporters were concerned, going on this afternoon.

As I waited for my turn to be questioned, I was so scared that my body was visibly shaking with my traitorous, icy-cold hands very much in evidence. Anyone who touched me would have thought I was dead and that no one had remembered to bury me. As I fidgeted with my papers, attempting as usual, a last minute review, I recalled how diligently I had studied for many weeks with great anticipation of this marvelous day. But would the senators ask me the things I knew and was so sure about? Or would they ask me devious questions in order to trip me up, giving them an excuse to deny me this opportunity, an opportunity I would have thought impossible for a person with no claim to fame such as me? I had spent a lifetime and a half in the classroom and I knew that anyone could prepare questions for success or failure depending on one's outlook or position on any given subject. I wondered what mood the senators would be in. I called upon St. Anthony to influence them to concentrate on the content that I knew so well.

As I wrestled with my insecurities, I reminded myself to talk very loudly when they questioned me so they could hear my responses. It would be so embarrassing if one would growl at me because he or she could not hear me. I recalled that as the introverted student I was, I would respond so softly when the teacher called my name during roll call that often the teacher would blurt out, "Well, are you or aren't you here?" I wasn't so sure I was all here today!

A thousand possible questions raced through my mind. "Wait! Why was I letting my thoughts wander when I should be getting back to reviewing all I had read, analyzed, memorized, synthesized, and in general, over-studied? But, darn it! Did I really know everything I was supposed to know?" I had often traveled throughout Latin America and although I had been to every other Central American country, I had never even made an airport stop in the Republic of Honduras. In my handbook, nothing equals firsthand experiences, and this created a void in my knowledge base. Would the senators quickly discover it and hound me for it?

Abruptly a thrust of loud noises bolted me out of my mental cocoon. The desk officer assigned to me by the State Department and I were sitting close to the aisle and as I turned, I saw that the oncoming stampede appeared to be none other than the media. It was like a tornado of human arms, TV cameras, regular cameras, notebooks, pencils, microphones . . . men and women, young and old. The spectacle, composed of many characters and things being shoved and pushed around, was anything but quiet.

I understood what the commotion was about when I recognized Governor Raúl Castro from Arizona in the middle of the fracas. He was the object of all their noisy attention. I had heard in the halls of the State Department that he was being considered for the ambassadorship to Argentina. Having seen him several times before on TV and in newspaper photos, I instantly recognized him. He was unruffled and as the experienced public figure that he was, pushed ahead, moving swiftly and confidently amidst all the TV cranes and flashes like a real pro, flashing a smile full of straight white teeth one could die for.

When he finally waded through the human ocean to the front of the room, the governor seated himself at that long, ominous table. He was joined by several other men attired in similar dark three-piece business suits. I had never seen them before, not even on television, and wondered about their identity. I realized I was seeing history in the making. There before the Senate committee were two Hispanics about to be interrogated for positions as ambassadors to foreign countries. Now that was indeed rare in our country! One was already famous with the media thick around him, but the other was a shoemaker's daughter with no fame, no media surrounding her, and no idea why she thought she could take on this new challenge in her life. When everything finally quieted down, as if on cue, two large doors magically opened behind the immense desk, and the senators and their staffs walked in and took their respective seats. As soon as they were all seated, the session was formally opened and a few questions and several remarks, all friendly and extremely polite, were directed at the governor. I kept hoping for a long question and answer session so the experience would help prepare me for mine, which was to follow immediately. I wanted to know exactly what to expect when my turn came up.

Not knowing which senators would appear at my hearing, I hoped that these same ones would remain. They appeared so caring and friendly with the governor that maybe I would get treated the same. After all, Castro and Jaramillo were both Spanish surnames. John Sparkman, Case Clifford, Dell Clayburne, George McGovern, Frank Church, Hubert Humphrey, Dick Clark, Joseph Biden, John Glenn, Richard Stone, Paul Sarbanes, Jacob Javitz, James Pearson, Charles Percy, Robert Griffin, and Howard Baker were the members of the Committee on Foreign Relations that ended up interviewing me that day, and I highly respected them because I knew they were individuals of the world who knew everything there was to know about it.

Much sooner than I had hoped, the questioning of the governor was over and the media commotion started again. The governor was leaving with hearty, boisterous congratulations from the senators and the many people who were surrounding him. I actively joined in the thunderous applause and wished I could touch him and wish him well as he went past me.

I didn't know if I would receive even minimum media coverage, but I suspected I would not. Few people in Washington knew who I was. Ever the timid shoemaker's daughter, I was extremely grateful for no publicity.

When everything was silent again, my name was called and I took my seat at the intimidating table, dashing, instead of walking, as was my usual fashion. I was in total awe and still remained in sheer fright. I am five feet six inches in height, tall for a Mexican American woman of my era, but I felt tiny and vulnerable at that huge table. Because of the formidable size of the furniture, the senators' names and reputations, and my fear, the senators seemed far away from me, sitting at a much higher level. I didn't realize until years later when I returned to that same room that they had been sitting on the same level I was. No eye-level dynamics here, a skill I had mastered and used to my advantage in my classroom.

Unexpected and abruptly, running footsteps broke the uncomfortable silence, and I turned to face Senator Pete Domenici and Congressman Manuel Luján, who had come to accompany me. They whispered that they had been delayed by a last-minute vote as a form of apology for being late. I didn't know either of them personally, nor did I know they attended these types of sessions, but I was more than pleased that these New Mexican politicians had joined me for support. I didn't recall ever having seen them up close or meeting them formally, but a fleeting thought entered my head that now there were three Hispanics! Putting my modesty aside, I put myself on the same political level as them. We were a governor, a congressman, and an ambassador . . . all Hispanics, and all from the Southwest . . . and in the same room in Washington, D.C., at the same time. Wow! What an experience.

The senator and congressman were friendly and they hugged me and wished me well. This small amount of excitement and movement warmed me up a little bit and I was able to stop the visible shaking, convinced that I appeared much more the confident professional. You can imagine someone being interrogated by a Senate committee shaking like a quaking aspen. That wouldn't make much of a positive impression, I'm sure.

When all the senators had again taken their seats during the brief interruption, my session was called to order. Before commencing, the visiting senator and congressman told the committee some flattering things about my being an exemplary New Mexican. It was a nice beginning for the exciting experience I was about to embark on—if I did well and survived today's hearing.

The senators asked me very routine, almost elementary school-type questions of geography and history. I answered them easily. But as always, I had prepared much more than necessary and I thought the questions should be much more difficult if this were truly serious business for our country.

The questions were simple and far too easy. "What language do they speak in Honduras?" I responded with the exact percentage of each of the various languages spoken. They asked, "What is the population?" Again, I answered without a flaw. But I was still terribly afraid that I wouldn't do as well as the standard I had set for myself. Ever the perfectionist, I had convinced myself that if they asked me my name, I would probably not know it. I wished my brain would settle down and not play any more games with me. I was supposed to focus on the topic at hand, just as I always told my students to do. I didn't know how difficult my own advice was to follow until that very minute.

I was slightly troubled that several of the senators were standing up and leaving, as were their corresponding staff members who sat behind them in the row of chairs directly in front of the large doors. It reminded me of the legislative sessions back home. People in and out, regardless of the business at hand. I had taken my second-graders to the legislative sessions several times during my teaching career, and was well acquainted with the legislators' behavior. I kept reminding myself that their leaving was in my favor; I would only have to impress and please those who remained. The fewer the better. My math seldom fails me.

After what seemed like forever, the chairperson asked if there were any more questions from his fellow senators. Each one replied there were no more and then they all smiled, congratulated me, and wished me well on my new assignment. My own New Mexican delegation, who had remained seated at the table with me, had to return hurriedly to cast another vote when the session ended, so the hugs and kisses were on the run, even before I had moved away from the table.

I left the room accompanied only by the desk officer. There was no fanfare for me, although a few friends had taken seats while I was responding to the questions. My husband had not been able to come. I could almost hear my own footsteps because the room had stilled so quickly. As we walked down the corridor, I wondered, Mari-Luci, what are you doing here? Did I really belong here? Was this position too far removed from the university setting where I was so happy, so comfortable, and so secure? Would people still listen to my ideas? I knew there would be no more captive audiences like those I had on campus. But I felt so strongly that we, as a nation, did not treat the Latino countries with dignity, and if I ever had a chance, I wanted everyone to know how wrong that was. So what if they were mostly small nations and the majority were extremely poor? I had been raised in a poor family too. I experienced firsthand the way many Americans viewed and treated the poor Latinos. After all, my father was Mexican and my mother was of Spanish descent, so some Americans felt I wasn't quite American enough. I had felt the division all my life from the two different sides of my hometown, one side consisting of the lighter-skinned people, and the other side belonging to those whose skin looked much darker like mine. We were often completely isolated from the Anglo children in school. Despite the fact that my skin was darker, my last name was Jaramillo, and Spanish was my first language, I was just as good an American as the next person and I should be treated as such. All peoples, Latinos included, should be given genuine respect regardless of their background.

I knew I was again getting agitated with my own thoughts on human rights, so I reminded myself to take one step at a time in this upcoming new experience. But I still wondered if I would be able to make a difference. Oh, God, maybe I should quit now before it was too late. Was the daughter of a poor Mexican shoe-maker really ready to become the first Mexican American woman ambassador to a Latin American country? The world and I would find out soon enough.

amily Life and Pancho Villa's Bugler

Las Vegas—not the glitzy, grandiose, cosmopolitan one, but the original Las Vegas—a small unpretentious and poor town nestled at the foot of the Rocky Mountains in northern New Mexico, was my birthplace. Las Vegas, meaning "the meadows" in Spanish, was founded by the Spanish around 1835. Although it was one of the most remote Spanish settlements, this small community ultimately grew up, becoming a bustling larger town on the Santa Fe Trail. It became the main thoroughfare for goods being exchanged from Mexico City all the way to St. Louis, Missouri. But despite its growth, Las Vegas still shows signs of its humble origins. The Plaza, which was a circular public gathering place, still retains its original design. Walls surrounding fields made of flat rock that were built more than two hundred years before were maintained by the current owners of the properties. Adobe brick *casitas* (little houses), many trimmed in blue to honor the Blessed Mother, held copious amounts of geraniums in windows and had patches of hollyhocks in the front yards.

These casitas were preserved by the traditional plastering of the exterior and interior walls with mud. Established on the west bank of a small river, the town spread and became divided in half by a small trickle of water called the Gallinas River. While gallinas means "chickens," the river was named for the flocks of wild turkeys found further upstream. This insignificant but vital source of water, which occasionally flooded in the spring, was the curtain that divided the town into two entirely different communities. Very small traces of that division remain today.

When I was a toddler and still learning to walk, Las Vegas was a community of at least four distinct groups of people. As I grew older, I recall hearing much about how we were grouped. Anglos and Jews, which were normally grouped together, were on top of the socioeconomic scale. Syrians ranked next. They were called "Turcos" by the local Spanish Americans and while being fairly economically successful, they were sometimes looked down upon by the upper class. Last in line came most of the town's founders. Many, but not all, ranked lower on the social and economic scale. A few were very wealthy. They called themselves "Spanish Americans."

The eastern part of Las Vegas was considered the Anglo side of town. It was prosperous and had more businesses. The Anglos had come with the railroad and built in the area nearer the train station and roundhouse. While Las Vegas had originally been part of the Santa Fe Trail, the coming of the railroad had turned it into a larger, more important commercial center. The native Spanish American population, which had already established Las Vegas on the west side, struggled with the influx of Anglo, Jewish, and Syrian businesses that flooded the town. But despite being dominated by the Anglo Americans, the Spanish language and culture persisted as a vibrant and strong influence.

Bridge Street was the main street on the west side. There was a theater and some large department stores where people went to buy their goods. These stores were controlled mostly by Syrians. The banks, the majority of which were located on the east side, were owned mostly by the Jewish community as well as several of the other businesses. Everything was divided.

There were two governments, two school systems, and two fire units. Even though there were two main bridges crossing the river connecting the town, the separations remained. There was a small amount of integration between the two sides of the river. A few Anglos lived on the west side and there were small pockets of Spanish Americans living on the east. I was born on the east side in a small house on Gallinas Street in one of those pockets, but despite the fact that we were on the east side, we were extremely poor.

I remember very little of my childhood in that first house; only the big elm tree crashing through our roof during an early spring storm and the Spanish American girl down the street that bit my hand, leaving a scar I still carry today. When I turned five, we moved to a house on Second Street, still on the east side, that my father, "Papito," had built. That's when things become clear in my memory and the language, culture, and traditions my father had brought with him from Mexico really began influencing and having an impact on my life.

Papito came from Durango, Mexico, when he was a teenager. Durango was at that time a medium-sized city in northwestern Mexico. Dad had been a bugler for Pancho Villa during the Mexican Revolution. General Pancho Villa was a revolutionary leader during the fight against an oppressive government. Dad had enthusiastically joined the revolution like all the other young men who were enticed by the troops marching through the towns in all their pomp and glory. He had no regrets, because he was leaving behind no immediate family except for one younger sister. All his uncles, with the exception of one, and his cousins, died during Mexico's revolutionary struggle. When Pancho Villa's troops found themselves in Juárez, near the U. S. border at El Paso, Texas, my dad couldn't help getting caught up in the American dream. Finding a Mexican circus that needed a trumpet player and was ready to conduct a tour in the southwestern part of the United States, Papito easily obtained the legal papers to cross the border. When the circus arrived in northern New

Mexico several months later, Dad left the group to seek his fortune in Las Vegas.

Despite his young age and his having suffered the loss of the influence of most of his male relatives during the revolution, he had already developed into a multitalented individual. Being an accomplished musician, electrician, inventor, and master leather craftsman, he chose to set up a shoe shop. He was quickly discovered and appreciated by the community for the beautiful boots, shoes, and saddles he made for the ranchers in the area.

My father, Maurilio, was a very handsome man. He was at least five-foot-ten, tall for most Mexican men in those days, and quite thin. He considered himself a "ladies' man," so he took care of his appearance down to the last detail. His pencil-thin mustache was always perfectly groomed and his mass of curls was always set "exactly so" on his forehead. Back then, men wore hats. Dad was very handsome in a hat and always tipped it for the ladies. Those curls wouldn't move a fraction of an inch under that hat. He had a lot of pizzazz.

I have no idea how much money he spent on himself, but I remember that my dad always had nice clothes. My mom would defend him by telling the family, "It's because he is constantly in public and has to be out with the band." And even though he would be covered from head to toe with shoe polish while at his shoe shop, those clothes also had to be appealing because he was meeting the public. Since he made his own shoes, they also were nice.

My whole world when I was five years old encompassed only the house Papito built for us, the dirt road we lived on, the school up the street, the park down the street, and our trips to the grocery store that was within walking distance of our house. Papito built our humble house from adobe. Adobe bricks were made by hand back then by packing mud and straw into wood frames laid in fields where they would bake in the heat of the sun. They would be stacked with mud between as mortar, and when finished, the walls would be plastered with additional mud protecting the bricks from the elements. Our casita had a tiny living room and dining area, a little kitchen, a tiny hall, and two small bedrooms. I don't know how we got it, but the one elegant thing we had in our home—other than Dad's musical instruments—was a beautiful chandelier that hung in the dining area. Miniature windows let in very little light, making our house always dark inside. There was no bathroom in the house, and our entire plumbing system was comprised of a pipe of running water with a bucket on the floor to catch the drips in the kitchen. Our outside toilet, called "el común," was complete with mail-order catalogs for wallpaper and toilet paper. This was a great way for us to always have reading material at hand.

Only my mother's natural ability to turn scraps into beautiful art saved our home from dreariness. She would cut tissue paper into doilies, embroider the pictures printed on flour sacks, or crochet anytime she could find a piece of thread. Hand-me-downs from other people along with flour-sack cloth would magically become coverlets for the beds, pillows for the couch, or even clothes for the family. She had a green thumb and obtained bits of plants from neighbors, filling our house with lively plants and flowers and turning the dark, tiny house into a home.

Mom also made the outside of our home delightful. She would plaster it with mud on a regular basis, repairing the gaps created by the changing weather. She was also bound and determined that we were going to have a lawn. Every morning she would get up early before anyone else and turn all the dirt in front of the house. She would take all of us and my brother's wagon to a natural meadow that was close to the house. The meadow was filled with grass and flowers and she would cut up little blocks of that meadow and bring them back in the wagon to plant in the yard. Before long, we had a lawn. She would ask people for bush roots and plant them all around the house and borders of the property. Soon lilacs filled the air with a beautiful scent when they were blooming in full glory.

I remember that we didn't have a lawn mower. When the grass started growing, my mother would go out when the sun had just started to come up and cut the whole lawn with scissors. Her example taught me a lot about perseverance and patience and that "where there's a will, there's a way." I'm sure Mom was probably embarrassed that we had no lawn mower, but because she loved beauty, she found a way. She always found a way. I believe that in later life, she fully understood how I learned from her to "make my way" and that "making my way" led me to that Senate hearing room.

I have an idea that she worked hard to make a lawn so we could play and not get so dirty. But I'm sure it was mostly because she loved for things to look pretty. We would come home from school, changing out of our nicer school clothes immediately, or return from playing and never know what to expect. She would rearrange the little bits of furniture we owned or find an orange crate and cover it with a cute little skirt and use it as a table.

My mother's ancestors were mostly from some of the pioneering Spaniards who had helped settle New Mexico. Mom was a beautiful, fair-skinned, rosy-cheeked woman, very different in looks from her handsome, olive-skinned husband. She was five-foot-five, unusual for that time period, much taller than most of her relatives and friends. My sister, at four-foot-eleven, was much more typical of Spanish American women.

Mom's long hair was always braided around her head or in a Spanish knot at the nape of her neck. Her natural thinness didn't quite match her round hips, but her traditional style of dress complemented her figure nicely. Her gathered skirts were made of flour sacks or hand-me-downs. She wore white blouses she made herself with ribbon, elastic, and occasionally embroidery at the top. Her shoes were always flat and simple. She never wore makeup or cut her hair. I guess you could say she was very old-fashioned, but that was because the Mexican influence introduced by my dad was more predominant than the Spanish

American influence she had grown up with. The old Spanish saying, "El hombre en la calle . . . y la mujer en la casa," (the man in
the street . . . and the woman in the house), fit their relationship
perfectly. His domination of the home was complete. He was
always served his meals first, my mother hovering around him
waiting for him to finish. After appeasing his appetite, Papito
would leave the table, which would be our signal that we could
then sit down and eat with our mother.

As I said, she was never allowed by her husband to wear
makeup or stylish clothes, or cut her hair. But the traditional
ways he brought from Mexico went even further. As children, we
never, never had a voice in any matters concerning ourselves or
the family. We were seen and not heard, which spilled over into
our behavior when first exposed to other aspects of everyday life
outside the home.

Mom's parents, neither one of them formally educated, eked
out a living by performing odd jobs and growing as much of their
own food as they could. Mostly they harvested beans, corn, and
small amounts of wheat. In the winter, my grandfather worked
cutting ice blocks in the dams north of Las Vegas in picturesque
Gallinas Canyon. Grandma did all the household chores that
women performed back then and bore a large number of children. Most of them died at birth or when very young. Five girls
did survive though, Mom being the youngest one of them.

When my mom, Elvira Encarnación Ruiz, was born, everyone thought Grandma was going to die because of the hemor-
rhaging she had suffered during the birth. Because of this, Mom
was given to her oldest married sister to be raised. Mom grew up
thinking of this sister, Juanita Ruiz, and her husband, Silviano
Tafoya, as her parents. And just as they were Mom's parents, I
grew up knowing and loving them as my grandparents.

It was this grandmother, really my aunt whom we called
"Nanita," who taught me to read Spanish prayers at the age of
five. She was always talking or praying out loud to God and the
saints. Rosaries and statues of saints were scattered all over her

house and a saucer of holy water rested on a small table near the entrance to her home. We would dip our fingers into the holy water and bless ourselves, making the sign of the cross on our chests as we came and went from her home. The doorways were blessed with this same holy water whenever there was a storm, and the garden tools became crosses in the yard in the event of lightning so no one would be hit. My days at their home were filled with gathering tubs of flowers from the fields for processions in the church on Sundays, and in the fields asking God for rain. Never ignored, flowers always needed replacing at the small shrines all over their property which were made from natural crevices in the rock where a small statue or picture had been placed. I was always Grandma's helper when it was time to clean the church, and her renditions of the *cánticos*, Spanish hymns, while we were cleaning, still echo in my mind today. Her habit of mentioning some saint in every sentence became my habit. My favorites quickly became St. Anthony, St. Jude, St. Francis of Assisi, and the Blessed Mother, whom I still call upon daily to assist me in my endeavors.

Grandpa was a stocky, fair-skinned, hazel-eyed, handsome man. He was a hard worker on his farm and helped everyone who needed help by digging a well, pushing a car out of the ice and snow, or helping plant fields. He loved all of us children and often covered for us when we did something wrong. When Mom would complain about our behavior, he would put his book down, perch his glasses on the tip of his nose so he could look at us better and say, "Behave, or I'll spank you tomorrow." Grandpa was a wonderful public speaker and very active in Democratic county politics. He was dubbed "Lengua de Plata" (silver tongue).

When the Democrats were in power in San Miguel County, he would be named probate judge. Those were the few times he had a salaried position and we would actually get store-bought clothes and lots of good food, including my favorite treat, bulk peanut butter. He kept our family together until my sister graduated from high school and took over the support of the family.

My grandparents' little farmhouse, which they had bought through a government loan when I was small, was in Sapello, a rural community that lies about twenty miles north of Las Vegas. It was an all-day one-way trip for us on a dirt and gravel road because we mostly walked. Sometimes we managed to hitch a ride with neighbors and friends, enabling us to spend more time with them on that particular visit. So since it was difficult for us to go to them, they would come to us often, sharing the fruits of their labors.

I remember them leaving behind the horse-drawn wagon and embracing progress by buying a Model T with a rumble seat. Grandma, Grandpa, and my sister would sit in the front seat. My mother, my brother, and I would ride in the open back of their black wonder of technology.

While I only experienced my grandparents' living in Sapello, Mom's childhood was spent in another small rural area called San Antonio, three miles north of Las Vegas on the north fork of the Santa Fe Trail. She did not receive much schooling. She had quit school in the seventh grade, but had at least learned all the "ins" and "outs" of homemaking. These would be severely put to the test over and over during her entire lifetime.

Even though she had only a seventh-grade education, she constantly reminded my sister, my brother, and me that a formal education was the only thing that would get us out of the extreme poverty we lived in. She had blind faith in education. Her belief later became the solid base of my entire career and lifestyle. I was delighted that she was still well and saw me receive my Ph.D. on graduation night. I ended up wanting the same educational opportunity for everyone I met. I became a teacher solely because there were no other career options at the time in my small home-town, but my mother's admonition that education breaks the poverty cycle was so embedded in me that I tried to learn everything I possibly could. Learning became my way of life.

Mom and Dad were married a year or so after Dad had come to town and set up his shoe shop. Elvira, my older sister, was born first. I followed seven years later and my brother, Maurilio junior, was born two years after that. We were raised in a bicultural home with subtle differences in the Mexican and Spanish subcultures in our house. The voice that my aunts had in their homes was never a privilege my mom knew. Papito's total domination overrode any of the rights she should have had like the other women of her day. Dad was the only native Mexican in town for many years, so there was lots of finger pointing at us for being "different."

Yet, owing to Mom's heritage, we knew we belonged. Because of Dad's influence, our Spanish language skills were much more developed than those of most of our friends. We also knew much more than our peers about Mexican culture, including its history and customs. We ate foods that others did not eat. Tamales were our favorite. At Christmastime, Dad always became generous and would buy the pork and corn needed to make them. We would have to bleach the corn with lye, wash and wash and grind and grind it. It was hard work, but worth it because it was the one time each year that we could give back to my mother's family some of the generosity they shared with us throughout the rest of the year. We would share our tamales with them and my mother eventually taught them to make their own. In a small way, it was the beginning of the Mexican food revolution that has spread across America today.

Pinole, a hot drink made from roasted ground corn, was another favorite treat. Enchiladas were common at my home, but few Las Vegans at that time ate corn tortillas and therefore missed out on that treat. Back then, that was one of the distinguishing Mexican practices my family had. Now you can't find a man or woman in Las Vegas that doesn't know how to make tamales and enchiladas and eat them three times a week, whether that person is Spanish American, Mexican American, or Anglo.

We spoke only Spanish at home. My mother spoke the Spanish from New Mexico. This particular Spanish had evolved very little beyond that of the Spanish settlers who originally brought it. Mixed with English words and intonations, it developed into a dialect of its own. On the other hand, my father had a much more cosmopolitan and literate vocabulary. His Spanish was beautiful and I loved its refined sound from the very beginning. Because of my dad, when I later began conversing with educated professionals from Colombia, Ecuador, and other Latin American countries, my early poverty could never be detected. He had passed his gift of polished language on to me.

I began school using Mexican Spanish while the other kids were speaking New Mexican Spanish. We didn't quite understand each other. When we did, I thought my words were prettier. I remember playing on the school's swings, yelling at another child, *"Empújame"* (push me). All the kids started laughing. One little girl said, "You mean *pushe*." This is an English word with a Spanish ending and Spanish pronunciation.

I said, "Yes," and quickly learned pushe. After saying it at home once, Father quickly straightened me out as to which word was correct. I became trilingual. I was learning the Spanish that my father wanted us to learn, the New Mexican Spanish of my community, and English at school. Looking back as an adult, I think that's what led me to my love of languages and the belief that everyone should be exposed to many of them. How fortunate to learn more than one.

Dad caught on early about the discrimination toward Mexicans, so he taught us to know the rich language, art, culture, and music of the Mexican people. You didn't hear in the United States about all the wonderful things that Mexico had. At that time, you never heard anything about a mariachi, a singer of ballads, in Las Vegas, although today they are found everywhere. As a result, when I was a youngster and was called a "dirty Mexican" by a Spanish American who, at the moment for whatever reason was mad at me, I knew I was spotlessly clean, scrubbed until my skin hurt, and that Mexico was a beautiful place with a rich history and tradition. I was learning to negotiate my way in a multicultural world, knowing how to behave and survive both inside and outside the home. Little did I dream these were my tottering, beginning steps in becoming a citizen of the world. No wonder I understood as an adult how to move amongst those cultures in order to negotiate successfully for what I wanted or believed in. I also had learned to appreciate the beauty in the different cultures I later encountered in my various careers.

My older sister, Elvira, and younger brother, Maurilio, and I were very close. Maurilio was the center of attention. He was a beautiful child with fair skin and rosy cheeks, and we adored him. We would bathe and dress him the best we could and carry him around even when he began to walk. Elvira and I were alike only in the darkness of our skin. She was tiny compared to my mother and me, but in every sense an enticing young woman. Her skirts always swayed when she walked, and her silky, feathery hair floated about her head like a miniature cloud because of the waves she inherited from our father.

Our next-door neighbors on the north side were as poor as we were. The father worked with a rancher and once in a while he would bring us some of the meat he brought home. We always got some of the lesser cuts such as hamburger or soup bones, but never complained about such a delicious treat. It was payment for my mother's help with his wife's chores of washing and ironing. I can still envision my mother heating the huge tub of water outside over a wood fire. She would carry the heavy buckets of heated water one at a time to the tiny back porch, or on a cold day, the kitchen. Scrubbing on a washboard in one tub and rinsing in another, she would occasionally sit, resting from the pain in her legs caused by varicose veins before hanging the laundry outside to dry. Ironing came last, heating the old-fashioned iron on the wood stove. There was no money exchanged, ever. I was seeing firsthand the barter system which I would later use to my advantage.

Eventually, we acquired neighbors on our south side as well. My mother ended up doing their laundry also. I'll never forget the reasons behind her labor-intensive work. It came about as a result of mom's allowing one of us kids to go to a school activity despite my dad's strict policy of no participation in extracurricular activities. My sister's senior picnic was held at Hermit's Peak, a nearby mountain, which was the tradition. To Las Vegans, Hermit's Peak had a special mystique surrounding it. It had a unique skyline that looked like a man's reclining head. With little imagination, you could see his forehead, nose, and chin. Some said there was a hermit who had lived there in caves at the summit, and some even claimed to have known him. While climbing toward the elusive caves, someone loosened a boulder, which tumbled down the mountainside and struck my sister in the head. Her skull was broken.

Being poor, we couldn't afford medical services. That's where one of our other neighbors came in. He was an Anglo doctor with a young, beautiful wife and a heart of gold. He would come over every morning to take care of my sister. We paid him by doing his laundry and cleaning his house. Her recovery was miraculous, considering the fact that she still has a hole in her skull today the size of a quarter. Mom never complained about her extra labors. She did it out of love for us and somehow, despite the time it took to do the laundry and house cleaning, we were kept fed, cleaned, and loved. As for the doctor, he was one of the few Anglos I had experienced in my youth that was kind to those with less than himself. I would get to know many more as I grew up.

Our family had lots of problems, not only those brought on by poverty. It was when Maurilio was still a baby that our father started leaving the house all night or for entire weekends. I didn't think it unusual at the time; I just thought that was the way all fathers were and accepted his absence with the trust of a child. My father, brilliant and hard-working as he was, shared very little of the small amounts of money he earned with his family. He had a roving eye and I'm sure having an extra "friend" on the side was all he could handle monetarily. The Spanish had a special word for this behavior, *casa chica*, meaning "little house" in English. I'm sure Dad's extra friend's house was as poor as ours.

Beyond this slight flaw of character, he was my personal example of a studious person and a scholar. He taught himself English and always, regardless of the task at hand, had a paperback book by his side and read at every opportunity. He had only brought a fourth-grade education from Mexico, but he was superbly self-educated and well read. And because of his own learning standards, he stood for no nonsense from his children and expected them to be superb scholars also. We were to bring home straight A's on our report cards. We never doubted for one moment that he was serious. We always came home with the highest marks given in our classrooms. I was a straight-A student from the very beginning of my schooling.

But although Dad was the example of the scholar, Mom was the one who made learning possible in our impoverished home. She insisted we do little house or yard work so that the free time my sister and I had could be used for studying. The exception was my poor brother, who had to go work in the shoe shop after school. The traditional gender role training started early in our home.

When we weren't studying, we read. My favorite stories were of Nancy Drew's adventures. The blue covers were easy to spot in the library and as I finished one book, I would race back to the library for the next, telling my friends all about her escapades in the process. Mom would occasionally send us for short periods of time outside to play. After all, she realized we were kids too and couldn't read and study all the time. But she was very protective and wanted us to be within eyesight, which meant we had to stay in view of her kitchen window or door. It wasn't until we were in school and started making friends that we would go off to someone else's house to play. But even then, we had a time limit and there was never any hanging around or going to town.

If Mom had only known about our adventures on the towers where the firemen used to practice, she would not have let us go outside at all. We'd go way up to the top, at least six stories high, and run down again. We had a lot of fun on those towers. As we got older, we would go to the local high school and play ball. That was the only limited way we were allowed to interact with our friends other than during the school day.

Despite all our physical activity, I wasn't much of an athlete. I would rather read and embroider. Embroidery was an activity popular with the poorer folks. Fabric and thread were cheap and the results could dress up even the plainest blouse or tablecloth. My mom was an expert at making things beautiful with her needle. She passed her knowledge on to me and I shared it with my friends.

One friend in particular became as adept at making pretty things as I was—especially after we got caught in the park by the caretaker. While my friend and I spent most of our time playing with dolls and making them clothes, one day we chose to go to the park against strict orders. There was a large tree with a broken branch and when the caretaker started coming after us, we ran to my friend's grandmother's house and hid in her basement. That mean man followed us and knocked on her grandmother's door. When she answered, he said, "The two little girls that came in this house broke a tree branch and the city is going to make them pay for the tree."

I died a million deaths. Besides breaking the rules by playing in the park, I knew we had no money to pay for the tree that we didn't even break. As a small child, I could see everything coming apart. I prayed to Baby Jesus to help us. He must have heard my desperate prayers because the grandmother didn't know we were downstairs and the man never came back to make us pay for the tree. After that horrible experience, I took to reading and embroidering even more for entertainment.

We always had books around: school books, magazines that people either lent or gave us, and as soon as we were old enough to go to the library, we had those books also. The librarian fit the stereotype of those days with the gray topknot on her head that never moved an inch and round-rimmed glasses perched on the tip of her nose. She was constantly shushing us when we would giggle. The ambiance in the library was rich to me with its beautiful ferns, hundreds of books, and the huge globe of the world. I loved being there.

Books became my friends, I think partly because my dad was forever reading. His influence of habitually being with a book was a good model for me. But they also became my friends out of the necessity for silence during the early morning hours. That was because of Papito's habit of coming home late at night from being out on the town either with friends or playing at a dance, party, or other community occasion.

The house had to remain perfectly still. We learned to tiptoe and whisper, not making any kind of noise. If we made a noise, he would come out of his bedroom and then not talk for days on end. His silence was his most powerful form of discipline.

Dad had one bedroom and Mom and we three kids slept in the other. When my brother was still tiny, he slept with my mother. My sister and I slept together. Later on, there was a cot for my brother. Dad had his own room because he would sleep late. That was the best arrangement for my mother. It allowed her not to have to tiptoe in the bedroom.

I don't ever remember Mom and Dad fighting. What I do remember was the silent treatment. And the silent treatment would happen often. He controlled the family with it. If he got quiet, we all got quiet. He was a controlling figure whose wife and children all obeyed. He never struck any of us except when I was five and my sister and I got into an argument. He popped our heads together. That was the only time I ever remember Dad using anything other than his silence as a discipline measure and punishment.

I never understood until I became a mother myself why my own mother didn't punish me more severely when I broke one of her few treasures, a little green tin holder with four green glasses that sat on top of the buffet in the dining area. We had very few beautiful things and I broke one of the delicate glasses while helping Mother clean one day. She spanked me and then forgave me. I remember wishing I had the money to replace it. I felt so sad and very guilty.

I recall my father having a piano in the house. It was one of many instruments that he owned. At the time, I never thought of it as a contradiction that he owned those expensive instruments and yet we had only beans and tortillas to eat. My sister took lessons on that piano, but by the time my brother and I came along, Dad didn't want us to have lessons. He said, "The musical world has become a world where everyone is out at night gallivanting around and I don't want you children to get into that." I realize now he was thinking about himself when he told us that. I have also since realized that if he had the money to buy such expensive things, he could have had the money to buy us the necessities of life that many others take for granted and that we did without.

Papito was the local musical genius. He wrote and arranged music. If people knew a song, he could transpose it for all the instruments in his band or orchestra. Sometimes he would bring men over to the house to play. Dad would compose a ballad about love or nature and then after introducing it to the other members of the band, he would play it beautifully on the trumpet while someone would accompany him on the piano. Occasionally he would get up late at night and we could hear the piano. He would tell us, "Las musas han venido," or in English, that the muses had come and he had to get the song out. He would write it out and spend most of the night working on it. I never inherited his gift of music and didn't learn to play, but music is ingrained in my very soul and oh, how I love to dance.

Grandpa made sure we learned how to dance at an early age. He would load Grandma, Mom, and the rest of us into his wagon and Dick and June, his horses, would take us three or four miles down the road to all the local fiestas. There he would make sure that all us little kids danced and danced and danced. I always got a kick out of how my grandpa bounced and moved around.

Polkas and waltzes were my favorites, that is, until years later when I would learn the *cumbia*.

Even though Dad neglected my musical education, I thought he was the smartest man in the world. His love of his culture, language, and music and the fact that his desire was strong enough to give that beauty to his children armed me with the power to succeed, despite the prejudice I was about to encounter in school. My mother's stubborn conviction that education was the road out of poverty became my driving force. My grandmother's foresight to teach me to read in Spanish at an early age enabled me to realize that I had the brain to learn everything I could possibly get my hands on. My grandfather provided the caring, mild-mannered, kind, and charitable male role model I would have never experienced if he had chosen not to help raise us. And last but not least, my sister, Elvira, helped support our family so I could continue to learn. These special people with their subtle cultural differences and personal strengths prepared me for the not-very-kind but beautiful world I was about to encounter when I began my journey through a multiethnic school.

chapter

Negotiate and Barter

Even though I was a shoemaker's daughter, I didn't
have nice shoes. Our family made a pair of shoes last
a long time out of necessity. We did this by cutting
new soles out of cardboard every night to put in
them when our shoes had holes. We did not have
the money to buy new ones when we needed them,
so we made them last a long time. In the upper
grades, my sister and I even painted our shoes with
enamel paint used for painting woodwork so our
winter black shoes could be summer white ones.
Somehow we always managed despite the fact that
my feet were growing very fast. I have very big feet
now. While we wore a lot of hand-me-down clothes,
our shoes were not. They just got very, very old. So
when I showed up my first day of school speaking
absolutely no English, wrapped in a skirt made from
yards of material rescued from a discarded flour sack,
my shoes had their typical cardboard soles in place.

My skirt was topped off with a peasant blouse
made from the same flour sack material with ribbon around the neck and puffed sleeves meant to
fool the eye into thinking there was flesh on my
arms. These flour sack skirts and blouses along with
occasional hand-me-down dresses that almost fit
me quickly became my standard uniform for two

reasons: we were too poor to buy ready-made clothes and Mother was concerned about the way the other children teased me for being so skinny.

As I said before, Mom was very clever. She would put darts everywhere in my hand-me-down dresses so they would stay on me. Big sashes and bows tied in back, lots of ruffles and gathered skirts helped disguise my almost nonexistent body. After having been a chubby baby, I surprised our neighbors and friends by shooting up like a weed into the wisp that I had become when I went off to school on my first day. In fact, it seemed that the most weight I carried was the long, heavy braids which would eventually be allowed to grow past my waist. These I wore every day of my life until I finally rebelled in seventh grade with the flimsy excuse that they were the reason my shoulders were rounded instead of straight. I cut my braids off a little at a time; the consequence was my dad's long silence.

There was no choice of colors for our clothes. It was not even a matter of importance in our home. We couldn't afford for it to be. Coats were hand-me-downs and as a result, were always either too big or too small. The navy dress that would become my standard and only outfit my first few days as an ambassador until I was able to purchase other appropriate dresses would constantly remind me of these long-ago days when I had no color choices. But by then, I would not only have many choices, but my taste in clothes would grow immensely. I had watched and learned how successful women dressed.

I remember a lot of painful things that happened during my first year of school, partly due to understanding no English, let alone speaking it, and partly because we were so poor that I had not been exposed to many things others take for granted. But because I had no trouble learning and loved doing so, the negative events were frequently overshadowed by the excitement of adventure, exploration, and learning.

While it seems to me that my first-grade teacher was kind, I remember being humiliated many times that first year in her class. In the beginning, since I couldn't understand what was being said, when the teacher asked a question and the children raised their hands to answer, I raised mine too. I thought it was a game. I didn't understand what was supposed to happen—that is, until the day came that the teacher called on me to answer the question. All the other kids put their hands down and when I looked around, not knowing what came next, they laughed at me. I never told anyone how embarrassed I was. I just quickly learned how to cover up my lack of knowing how things were done, and I learned to over-prepare and pay attention to timeliness and detail. Later, most of us Spanish-speaking kids were moved to another classroom. There were way too many kids in the room, but the adults used the excuse that it was to keep us together for advice and counseling. I don't recall the advice and counseling, just the segregation, which was totally unnecessary.

While learning to read, write, and speak English, first grade also exposed me to some of the small luxuries my family couldn't afford. After recess, we would go back to our classroom and put our heads down on our desks to rest. While our heads were down, the children that could afford to buy milk got to go up to the front of the class and sit in a reading circle to drink it. A special day came for me when one of the little girls that had bought her milk in advance wasn't there. The teacher chose me to drink it. I thought it was the greatest thing to be allowed into the elite milk-drinking circle. I drank milk from a milk carton. I had never had that experience before and I still remember it vividly. As an adult, I still love milk, but now it is skim because my hips keep getting bigger and bigger.

By the time second grade rolled around, I had learned how to get by without the "extras" the other children were lucky enough to have. During an activity in which we were supposed to draw a picture in crayon, in my effort to do the best I could, I whispered to the little girl next to me that I would do something for her if she lent me her crayons. From that day forward, I never missed anything again. Whether my payment for borrowing was reading and highlighting in someone else's book so I didn't have to buy it, or tutoring, I did whatever I had to do to get through school. By mirroring my mom's skills, I had discovered the great use I could make of the bartering system. Unknown to me, I began developing negotiating skills which would be continually sharpened from bartering with fellow students. I used this new discovery of negotiating powers then and all the way through the university level. Bartering and negotiating became a way of life for me.

Second grade was also the year my dad bought a brand-new car. While we had to walk everywhere, my dad always had his car. It was for him to go to work at the shoe shop in the mornings and to have at night for either playing engagements with his band, or unknown to us, his other nocturnal activities. Once in a great while on Sundays, he would take us to the farm. Even though we would get to ride in the car, it wasn't a family car; it was Dad's car. I think that's why as an adult, through the years, I have always owned snazzy cars, including two Mercedes Benzes and a Lexus. I probably felt a need to always have a beautiful car that is mine because of the possessive behavior my dad exhibited.

Because Dad didn't share his car with us, we had to walk for groceries. It was OK though, because he only gave us small amounts of money at a time. That meant twenty-five cents of flour, ten cents of beans, ten cents of chile, and ten cents of sugar . . . and very few packages to carry home. Everything was in open bins and the clerk would weigh it for us. Thank goodness for the simple ways of life back then. We never would have been able to afford the grocery stores of today.

We were too proud to let people know how poor we were. So since we had to go almost daily for our small amounts of food, we would scout for small sticks as we walked down the sidewalks. We always kicked them to remember where they were. This wasn't just children's play. There was a definite reason that we kicked them. We didn't want the neighbors to see us take them home. We would go back in the evenings to gather them for use in our house for both heat and cooking.

The local store owner liked us, giving us an occasional lollipop because we were very polite. Everyone was addressed with "yes, ma'am" or "yes, sir." One day, a rather refined-looking lady, who by chance was in the store while my brother and I were there for our daily purchases, turned to me and asked, "Are you Black?"

I looked at her light-skinned hand and replied, "Yes, ma'am." I was aware of the whispering behind my back as my fair-skinned brother and I left the store to go home.

I asked Mom when I got there if I was Black. She asked me what answer I had given the lady and I replied, "I said yes, Mama, because the lady was very white."

My mom hugged me and said, "No, sweetheart. There are people that are black-skinned and you are not a black-skinned person, you're a Mexicana." Our sheltered world was very small and we had no opportunities to be exposed to many of the wonderful varieties of life. It wasn't until years later when I was already out of junior high that I would finally see a Black person for the first time. That was when I finally learned what was really meant by being "Black."

Mom must have told Grandma about my conversation with the lady in the store because it was after that when every evening Nanita began treating my face, hands, and any other skin that would show outside my clothing with a tablespoon of wet, raw oatmeal wrapped in cheesecloth. She would tell me, "Estás muy ahumada." There is no way to accurately translate into English what she was saying to me, but in essence, she was telling me my skin was smoky. She believed her treatments would lighten up my skin to reflect the coloration of the rest of our family, but in the mornings when I would eagerly wake up to see the change, my skin would remain as dark as the day before.

It seemed part of my nature to want to "belong," not just with the kids at school, but with the Spanish American kids that lived near my grandparents' farm as well. I spent part of my summers with my grandparents. I loved the farm. With them I learned so much. Besides teaching me to read in Spanish, Grandma taught me how to share. She taught me humility and empathy. Grandma would see a neighbor coming from across the river and say, "Here comes our neighbor and her children. We have to add more water to the beans." Somehow there was always a warm bowl of something to eat at her house. No one ever went away without eating.

Even though Nanita was skilled enough to renovate her own hats, her talents didn't end with being just a housewife. It went much further than that. Nanita didn't reach a height of five feet, but she was anything but handicapped because of it. She was extremely strong. She never hesitated to hitch the horses to the wagon when Grandpa wasn't around. Nor did she balk at pushing their car out of the mud later when progress caught up with them. She hoed the garden, irrigated, and harvested. Grandma was traditional in most senses of the word, but she was never afraid to speak her mind. Her hair was always styled in the newest fashions and I wished my dad had allowed us this one small concession from being strictly traditional, although I thought of it more as old-fashioned.

At my grandparents' house, I discovered there were people who seemed even poorer than we were. Even though my shoes were torn and old, the farm children went barefooted. We would get out of my father's car and they thought we were rich. They would make snide remarks about "these town kids." I resented that because I knew that we were just as poor as they were. That's why I spent my summers with my shoes kicked off. I wanted them to see that I was just like them. I wanted to be accepted. I didn't want to be different or better. I just wanted to be friends. When we would play, I would race the kids barefooted also. I won many times, not because I was a great athlete, but because I was already developing long legs.

Despite the fact that I was friends with the farm kids, there was always an underlying competition between us. They always tried to prove that they knew more than us town kids. They had horses and one day one of the guys said to me, "My God, you're so big and tall and you don't even know how to ride a horse."

I said, "Sure I do! I've ridden on my grandfather's horse many times."

"Yeah, but your grandfather always leads the horse," he taunted.

I rose to his challenge and said, "I can ride a horse as well as you."

He said, "Try it!" I gulped down my fear and got on that saddle and the horse took off. I didn't know how to guide it, but was finally able to steer him back to where the kids were waiting. As I started to climb down, the saddle fell off. They had put on the saddle without the cinch and thought I would fall off right away. Their plans had backfired. Maybe because I was so scared and was clutching the horse so tightly, the saddle had not come down. "Gracias, San Antonio!"

Grandma helped me discover my faith in God. She offered prayers for everything she did and taught me those same prayers in Spanish. Through her and my mother's faith, Catholicism became deeply ingrained in me. I think I would probably have become a nun if I had known a Hispanic nun or priest as a child. As it was, I didn't see my first Hispanic priest active in the church until I was in my forties. But at least, the nuns quickly became my role models from when I saw them at the morning masses that Mom and I would sneak to at the Catholic school. I say "sneak" because Dad was an atheist and didn't allow us to go to mass. The nuns showed a kindness as teachers that I didn't often see at the public school.

Nanita also taught me the names of all the plants and weeds in the area. I have never forgotten them. Even as an adult, I remember the Spanish names but have never learned all the English ones. Grandma did know enough English to get by, but her second-grade education was a way out for her not to use her English skills. We would encourage her to speak in English and tell her, "Grandma, say 'robin.' "

She would reply, "No puedo decir 'robin,' es un 'robinsón.' "
In other words, she would tell us she couldn't say the word

"robin" in English and then she would repeat the same word in her Spanish dialect.

My grandparents were ahead of their time. They didn't have the vocabulary and didn't talk about the environment, but they were environmentalists and taught me to be the same. We would walk down to the river and see something that didn't belong there and pull it out because they wanted to keep the water clean. They refurbished the soil and put in logs and big rocks to prevent it from eroding. They taught me the things I would have never learned if I had just stayed in town. I became a gardener because they always gave each of us kids a little plot after we helped them with the large-scale farming. I loved turning the dirt, mud, sticks, and rocks into little roads and towns. We always had a few vegetables and flower seeds to plant on a small piece of land to call our own.

When I reached third grade, my teacher was quite strict, which made her appear mean, but my desire to be a pleaser assisted me in being an excellent student. During Halloween, she asked me to recite a poem I had written to her bridge club. Up to then, I had never done anything all by myself and I trembled with the sheer terror of speaking in front of her friends. I don't know if it was from anxiety that things would go wrong or if it was the fact that it was the first time I had to do something that wasn't in the secure environment of my family or the classroom. But I remember a feeling of great fear that stayed with me, encouraging my later development into a very shy person. I kept telling myself that in order to combat my fear I had to do well so my teacher would be proud of me. I read my poem to the ladies sitting at card tables, staring at the goodies and sweets that were assembled in front of them all the while to avoid eye contact with them.

They all clapped profusely when I finished. I remember feeling that it was really neat that they had liked my poem. My teacher asked me to go with her to the kitchen and there she put some jelly beans and one cupcake decorated with a Halloween motif in a bright orange napkin with a cat on it and gave it to me. I was so excited. I could hardly get home, running with that cupcake and jelly beans. It was a real treat for my family. We sat around the kitchen table and counted out the jelly beans, dividing them among my sister, brother, me, and Mom. We cut the cupcake into four pieces and had our first Halloween party. That left a big impression on me as young as I was. It was my first salary and my first attempt at doing something in a new environment. I had done my first public speaking.

While my second and third grade classes had been mixed with English-speaking kids and Spanish-speaking kids, fourth grade was a repeat of my first grade year when we had been put in classes according to our ethnic background. The English speakers in my fourth grade year had the principal as their teacher. We Spanish speakers had a different instructor. As an adult and a teacher myself now, I look back and wonder why we were separated this way. At that time, it was pretty much assumed that Anglo children were smarter and therefore, since the principal had other duties besides teaching, she was given those kids so she wouldn't have to spend so much time teaching concepts they wouldn't grasp right away. We were once again being segregated and while as children we didn't realize what was happening because everyone accepted everyone else, the adults were teaching us that we were different—different in an undeserved way.

There were many older boys in my fourth grade class because there was no social promotion. A grade would be repeated until the student mastered the subject matter. These boys had been in trouble and had been in reform school and in order to get out, had enrolled in our school. That's when I began to really become aware of the empathy I was developing for others. Those fifteen- or sixteen-year-old boys were forced to squeeze into tiny little chairs and desks with ten-year-old kids. I felt so sorry for them. The teacher seemed to enjoy embarrassing them by asking them questions they couldn't answer. They would turn beet red and I would get very uncomfortable for their sakes. Even though I knew I would be severely reprimanded at school and very likely beaten at home if I got caught, I got in the habit of giving them the correct answers to seat-work questions. I would write them on little pieces of paper and sneak them to the boys because I felt so sorry for them and hated to see them humiliated.

The friendship that developed with these boys worked to my advantage. My teacher was a very nervous type and often when the students misbehaved, she would have a fit, fainting and collapsing on the floor. I would run for the principal while the other kids stood surrounding her and gawking with their mouths open. Down the hall the principal would charge, yelling all the while for the students to get back in their chairs. The kids would sit down, the principal would fan the teacher's face, and pretty soon, she would get up. The principal would take her down the hall to rest until she felt OK. To this day, I don't know if those were some kind of epileptic seizures or something else. While the principal assisted her, I would be left in charge—I was the teacher. The principal trusted me because I was a good student and evidently showed leadership skills. As a grown-up, I think back and thank God that I was nice to those boys because they could have made my life miserable. But, because they were my friends, they would help me keep the room quiet and continue with their assignments until our teacher felt well enough to return to the classroom again.

I was used to being queen of the hill—few ever got grades as good as mine. But in fifth grade, I developed the true spirit of competition. I never had to take final exams because I would always top all the tests, earning that time off to read while others were taking their final tests. But at the end of our first six weeks, a short redheaded fellow challenged me for that privilege. All of a sudden I realized that this little guy was competing with me and try as I would, I couldn't get rid of him. Just as I'd answer a question, he would have to answer one and then another. We kept on trying to outdo each other, so the teacher finally gave up and declared a tie. It was the first time in my student career that another classmate besides me was allowed to skip the final exam. I decided then and there that I had to watch this one. I did not like this redheaded fellow challenging me for the top position in class.

So in fifth grade, shy and inhibited and afraid that I might do something wrong, I competed with this fellow. I would innocently ask him how much he read or how many problems he did so I could make sure that I read further and answered more questions than he. Everywhere else I was helping the other students and still sneaking them the answers. On the playground I was telling them what I felt sure the teacher was going to ask. I helped everyone except him, my first competition.

I really became conscious of something being horribly wrong when in sixth grade, we were so totally segregated from Anglos that we were made to stay on "our side" of the building at recess. The teachers were sometimes mean to us Hispanics, but especially with the boys. They would be hit with rulers and made to stay in at recess with their heads down. They sometimes weren't even allowed to go to the bathroom. I saw so many mean things in those years. Because I was a good student, I didn't receive that rough treatment, but I was kept from my Anglo peers just the same.

By the time seventh grade rolled around and I went to the junior high school, a complete division between the two groups of children had been created that had not existed before, even though now our classes were mixed again. Now all the Anglo girls joined Rainbow Girls, all the Anglo boys joined the DeMolay club, and most Spanish Americans didn't join any clubs. We didn't know what "Rainbow" or "DeMolay" meant. We just heard these names all the time. We thought those clubs were just for Anglos. From that time on, social activities between our two groups became separate. The system had succeeded in teaching the Anglo children prejudice and teaching us that we were not as good as they were. I realize now how wrong segregation was, but nobody spoke up about it then. Our adults were like oppressed people everywhere; they just didn't talk about their problems outside their small circles.

While Papito was often at home when I was in elementary school, he was rarely around later on. But even at a distance, he continued to remain a strong influence on us. We would be rewarded with a nickel or dime when we came home with straight A's on our report cards. He would tell us how smart we were and we would be floating on clouds. I loved him dearly and thought he was the smartest man in the world.

It wasn't until we were older that we realized our dad was never there as other dads were. There was always the wonderful excuse of his having to work at night to support us, but in reality, we received very little support from him. I felt stupid when I realized that he had "extra friends" and that everyone else knew.

Mom told me once, "Oh, sweetheart, people will always exaggerate. He has to have these contacts for his work." She shielded us as much as she could and eventually we just learned to live with the knowledge of his other side. I never became bitter toward my dad despite his tendency to seek out other company besides my mom and his little family of us three kids. My mom would always say, "There's someone hurting more than you and we have to help." So with Mom's gentle influence, that became our way and we always tried to be good citizens in the community.

While others would think my dad had his faults, he was extremely confident in himself and secure in his ways. His personal convictions reflected on us, teaching us children to be sure of ourselves, become educated, and be proud of who we were. His love and pride in his culture had indeed rubbed off on us and I never felt inferior to the Anglo kids at school.

His heart was a good one. There was something in the newspaper about a man from Mexico who had both his legs cut off in a horrible railroad accident, so being a fellow Mexican, Dad took him in. He wore artificial legs and a harness that my father made for him. He was talented with his hands and helped Dad a lot. He would play the guitar and sing beautiful Mexican songs and ballads. I was in high school when he died. I loved this man deeply. He represented to me the beautiful Mexico I had never seen and helped me build more pride in my Mexican heritage.

At his rosary, I cried and cried and cried. No one could understand my special attachment for him and my tremendous flow of tears. I was so frustrated with myself for wearing my heart on my sleeve, everyone seeing my teary eyes and red nose. But eventually I accepted my strong emotions and reactions toward the pain of others as a positive trait. His name was Salvador, meaning "savior." Indeed he was, in a manner of speaking, because at a time in my life when I felt the attitude toward me of some of my Anglo classmates that I wasn't as good as they were, he helped me to understand myself.

Dad's domination and influence in our lives despite his infrequent visits and support never really bothered me, for the most part. He did, however, try to prevent us from practicing Catholicism. His claim to be an atheist meant we still had to go to church in secret. Mother and I had continued to get up and go to early mass and be back before anyone missed us. Since we weren't allowed to go to catechism, Mom and Grandma taught us at home most of the time. I finally made my first holy communion at the age of twelve, about three years later than most Catholic children. My brother made his at the same time. He was ten. We just went to mass one Sunday and sat in the front row. The priest knew that my father was against Catholicism and didn't want us being Catholic, so our first communion was arranged after attending just a few classes.

I was still growing ever upward in my teens, but hardly outward. I was still scrawny and had by this time realized my awkwardness and outdated appearance. In rebellion against my father's strict rules and old-fashioned practices, I started chopping off my heavy braids. He couldn't change that, but I had to keep my fingernails clipped short and wasn't allowed to wear makeup. I couldn't figure out how to get away with letting my fingernails grow long like those of other girls, but I did get around the makeup. That was easy. I just put it on at the end of the block in the morning while walking to the junior high school and washed it off before I got home. My lips were always chapped as a result, but that was just part of growing up.

While I wasn't really interested in boys yet, I gained a very close friend who was a boy in seventh grade. I was taller than he and his skin was fairer than mine, but we were both "raza." Our class was planning a party and it was my job to call the dairy to find out how much ice cream cups would cost us. Because our teacher was also the principal that year, Spanish Americans and Anglos were together again and there was a telephone in our classroom. I didn't tell anyone that I had never picked up a tele- phone before, not even a toy phone. I had never even seen any- one talking on one. I went to the front of the room and picked up the telephone, holding it up to my ear. Before I dialed half the number to the dairy, a boy grabbed the phone and quickly turned it around in my hand saying, "Mari-Luci, that's the mouthpiece. That's where you talk." I had the phone turned around the wrong way. Needless to say, that boy earned my gratitude and respect immediately because he said it quietly enough that the other stu- dents nearby didn't notice. His dad was the chauffeur and gar- dener for a rich lady and he had had exposure to those "rich" kinds of things. I turned as red then as the red phone at my fin- gertips that I had available to call the president later at any given moment when I became ambassador to Honduras. No one picked up on it that day and to this day, I don't like using the tele- phone. I would much rather talk to people directly.

By the time I was in seventh grade, we had moved from our small adobe house to a two-room apartment on Railroad Avenue, which was only a few blocks away. Dad never spent any time with us in this small home. He had gone back to Mexico to seek his for- tune and fame. He had left us with only our clothes and other necessities. Nothing else was left behind for us, not even the chandelier from our adobe home. Piling all the equipment in his shoe shop beside all our household items in the back of a great big truck, he left with the promise that once his fortune was made, he would send for us. Being leery of such an uncertain future, I real- ly didn't feel much excitement for the prospects of what he was promising us. I just concentrated on surviving another day on our slim budget and getting good grades in school.

Staying there only a short time, we moved once again. This time it was to the basement of Dad's shoe shop after he returned from Mexico penniless. His vision of success had been swept from him with the coming of World War II. His attempt at fame and wealth in Mexico lasted almost two years. Despite the distance and time apart, he wrote to us and sent a few things. My prize possession was a pair of rattlesnake skin shoes that he made especially for me.

Two houses down from our new home was a bakery owned by a German American woman. She was an excellent baker even though she was very crippled and used a crutch under one arm and a cane in the other hand. She was not a handsome woman. She was large and had deformed feet, and children would cross the street and walk on the other side to avoid her because they were afraid of her. They would run away from her yelling, "Here comes the witch!" I felt so sorry for her and since my father's shoe shop was so near, I got to know her well.

Maybe because of her physical appearance, she had learned to be thrifty, realizing she would have to take care of herself in her old age. She knew there would be no husband or children in her future, only nieces and nephews. I used her as an example later in my own life to save a little of every dollar I earned. I witnessed the positive benefits of economizing when she was able to visit Rome.

I began cleaning her house and storefront for her. In the summer, I would wash the walls and scrub anything that could be touched by water. During the week, I would sweep and wash the kitchen floor. She even had me go down into the coal bin and scrub it too. For this I was paid the grand sum of fifty cents a week. Some might say it was exploitation, but I don't think it was. My fifty-cent salary was a lot of money for us at that time and she enlightened me in so many wonderful ways. I had never been exposed to things most people take for granted. She taught me to eat many things I had never seen before. German goulash became one of my favorites and canned tomatoes with salt was a vegetable but became a dessert if served with sugar, and yummy fruit cakes—yes, I love fruit cakes.

She even taught me how to make tea. She had carefully orchestrated refreshments that she planned to serve at her bridge club from the Catholic church that was meeting at her house one particular time. She arranged with me that I was to wait and when she signaled me, they would be ready for the tea. When the time came and she requested the tea, I immediately appeared with it. She was amazed and asked, "How did you do that so fast?" I said, "I made it a long time ago." Needless to say, the tea was black. I remember her shaking her head, rolling her eyes and telling the ladies they'd have to wait for the tea because I had spoiled it and she'd have to make new tea. So she taught me how to steep tea.

I loved her. She thought I was smart and good and, boy oh boy, was I a hard worker. I learned how to scrub and put my hands in almost boiling water. She always said that hot water was how you got things really clean.

Because so many children dropped out of school after six or seven years, eighth grade graduation was a big to-do. It was complete with diplomas, choruses singing, and a procession. Of course I didn't have a new dress to wear. I felt left out of the conversation and excitement the other girls shared when they would gather and talk about their new dresses. My friend and employer, the baker, asked me one day if I had a new dress to wear. When I said no, she said, "I have a beautiful silk dress I bought in Rome. If your mom wants to, she can undo that dress and make you a dress to go to graduation in." So I had a silk dress for graduation. To this day I remember its cream color and silky feel. The pink, pale yellow, and peach-colored dainty flowers with tiny leaves sprinkled all over it looked lovely with the Peter Pan collar and the still ever-present large sash my mother attached so I wouldn't fly away going up the stairs for my diploma. I felt very good about that dress and about graduating.

High school was quite a change for me. Spanish Americans were very much in the minority. You see, lots of us had been dropping by the wayside. The few of us attending high school were a nice bunch of kids, though. We were quiet and did what the teachers told us to do. We weren't any trouble except for an occasional fistfight between the boys.

I had a reputation of being an excellent student. I wore a little halo that said, "Give her an A." I really didn't have to apply myself to my schoolwork anymore; it just came naturally. I was very popular with the girls. I had lots and lots of girlfriends, but they teased me because I was so skinny. They had all developed and had beautiful bodies. I was still just skin and bones. Up to this time, I never had any boyfriends. I was just too skinny, ugly, and a bookworm to boot. The other kids loved my sense of humor, but because my eyeteeth hung over my bottom lip when I would smile or laugh, I always had a hand over my mouth so no one would notice my walrus teeth. Because of my many friends, I didn't notice the kids around me pairing off and that I was one of the few without a boyfriend.

With Spanish Americans being a minority, our school was very Anglo oriented. There was seldom any Spanish spoken unless it was in Spanish class. There was no overt pride or joy in being a Spanish American. There was no display of our practices anywhere around except in our own homes. It was a difficult time for us. We even hid our sandwiches at lunch if they happened to be made with a tortilla instead of bread, or we just wouldn't eat at all. Because of our upbringing, of being only seen and not heard, we had no idea whether our ways were acceptable to others or not. After all, when we were much younger, in elementary school, we had been separated from those children who were considered smarter than we. And as young adults, our parents still did not discuss these types of subjects with us.

After seeing one of my friends hiding a tortilla sandwich at lunch one day, I decided that if she was smart enough to bring a tortilla to school to eat at lunch, I would bring one too. The challenge for me was that I wasn't going to hide it! I wanted to see if there would be any consequences for actually showing something familiar only to us. I remember bringing out my tortilla, wondering what looks and comments I was about to receive. But nothing happened. Nobody said anything at all! I had tested the system to see where my boundaries as a minority might lie and the result was a realization that my culture could blend and be accepted by others not like me. That occasion was a sort of coming out for me. I decided that I shouldn't always be hiding in the shadows. I was getting braver and bolder. While I didn't go marching down the street holding a banner, I began to hold my head a little higher, square my shoulders a little more, and feel good about who and what I was. Little did I know that this was my training ground for my civil rights work later in life. I did not say anything to any of my friends about that special day, but I felt good about that tortilla and the tiny new step I had taken.

The school subject I loved the most was math. My math teacher encouraged me in more ways than any teacher before him. When he was quite old, I saw him and his wife at a dance in Albuquerque. He came right up to me, even after all those years, and proceeded to praise me as he had done in high school. He told me I was his best student ever, and I know I glowed as much from his praise then as I did the first time, fifty years before.

I became the algebra star for the school and if any visitors came to tour the school, they were taken to my math class where I was promptly sent to the board to do difficult algebra problems. I could do them as fast as my hand could write. I had memorized the formulas. It wasn't until I took geometry in my second year of high school that I finally discovered a subject I had to work at. I worked very hard that year to get my good grade but I didn't like the subject. Since there was no tutoring or counseling, I chose never to take a math class again. Something happened to me that year. I realized that there were subjects I didn't like studying. My dislike of the math world after my geometry experience has stayed with me. I turned down many wonderful job opportunities when I found out I'd have to be involved with finances and dreaded spreadsheets.

At about this time, I started taking other kinds of risks. I was still very shy and would shake when I had to go to the front of the classroom. I didn't feel very assertive yet, but when I was advised not to take Spanish because I already knew the language, I took it anyway. Perhaps it was because I was told not to or perhaps from curiosity about the Anglo teacher who was teaching it. Her pronunciation for almost everything was very "English," especially her double L's. I knew her Spanish pronunciation was terribly wrong but she always told the class that we were to never correct her because she spoke Castilian Spanish. Since none of us knew that Castilian Spanish is a dialect from Castile, Spain, we didn't object. She really elevated herself over us. I kept thinking that she was wrong because my father spoke beautiful Spanish and he didn't sound like her. But because I wasn't strong enough to speak up, I kept quiet. Of course I got an A+ in her class, but my language wasn't validated. Speaking Spanish was still a put-down and many of us felt that our language just wasn't good enough.

I began accepting several positions at school even though I was still very shy. I was either busy with the Spanish club or the Home Ec. club, or busy being in charge of other different activities. While I was changing inside, my appearance still was not changing much on the outside. I was still painfully thin. Nowadays I would have been accused of being anorexic even though I had plenty of energy and never suffered from even common ailments. But there just wasn't enough food at my house that appealed to me. I rarely felt like eating. We mostly had very soupy beans with an infrequent potato or some Spanish rice. On rare occasions there was a piece of meat, but it would be prepared in such a way that it would feed our entire family of three youngsters and two adults. I would drink a lot of water, gulping down two or three glasses before sitting down to eat, so I was seldom hungry. Times were as lean as ever at my house.

I transferred schools during my senior year in high school. We had moved once again to a small house that we built ourselves one adobe at a time after school and on weekends on Independence Avenue on the west side of town. This new home resembled our other small adobe house closely and I once again felt comfortable in a home that truly belonged to us. My high school was now too far away to walk to any more during the cold, snowy winters, so my brother and I were enrolled at New Mexico Highlands University Laboratory High School, much closer to our home. That was a wonderful experience for me. Classes were much smaller. All the kids there had been at that school for their entire school careers. Maurilio and I had to learn to make friends quickly and to hold our own. He was a sophomore and I was a senior. We were accepted quickly by our peers and the teachers, who were still all Anglo, loved us. I was only sorry that I wasn't cheering for my old high school, but felt I couldn't possibly cheer at my new high school.

Dad had never allowed us to go to football games or dances or any other extracurricular activities. That part of my life was completely void. But now that we lived near the school and Dad was gone so much, even though Mom was really scared to let us go, she would give my brother and me permission to go for a little while to some of the dances. It was only for an hour or an hour and a half and then we had to run home.

It was worth the risk. I loved to dance. Maurilio, who by that time was almost six feet tall always invited me to dance first and would make sure I was never standing against a wall unnoticed. A girl came up to me one day asking where I had gotten such a great-looking boyfriend. Few had realized yet that Maurilio was my brother. We laughed about that one. That year, I got to go to at least six or seven dances. We even got first prize for the best dance once. We loved to jitterbug and for the first time in my life, there were two or three boys interested in me. I was asked to attend the senior prom—a real date!

Right before graduation, my favorite teacher came to me and said, "I need to talk to you Mari-Luci." Off we went to her office. I had no idea what the matter was when she said, "I'm going to get right to the point. Why do you keep referring to yourself as Mexican?"

"Because I am," I said, not understanding at all what she was trying to get at.

She said forcefully, "You are not!" I insisted again that I was. I realized she was very serious when she said that I wasn't Mexican, but Syrian. Remember that there were a lot of successful Syrians in Las Vegas at that time. They were powerful families and widely accepted.

I said, "No, I am not . . . I am Mexican."

She sighed and gave up, saying, "OK. That's all I wanted to talk to you about." I left her office and even today it is a mystery why she wanted me to claim I was Syrian. Was I doomed because I was Mexican? If I had said I was Syrian, did she think I could go further with my life? Mexicans were still at the bottom of the heap in those days. I don't know if she was trying to create a better path for me or hinting for me not to be so vocal about being Mexican.

Graduation night finally came and I didn't know what the next day would bring for me. I knew I needed a job desperately but I didn't know what I was going to do. I never talked with my parents about my future. I supposed I would try to get a job at the state hospital, a large hospital for mental patients. It was one of two places in town that hired many Spanish Americans. The other one was the university. But both offered low-paying staff positions. In those days, we didn't find many Spanish-speaking physicians and/or professors. I also could apply at Newberry's, the local five-and-dime store. I was full of anxiety but not very forward looking.

I was shocked when my father showed up for my graduation ceremony. He had never attended anything I had ever been involved in. It was at Ilfeld Auditorium at Highlands University. Its beautiful red façade and burgundy velvet seats inside made it by far the most prestigious building in town. Our graduation class consisted of twenty students. We sat down on the stage after marching in wearing caps and gowns, the whole works. Award time came and I was called for all the awards. One award was given to two people but even then they called my name first. The crowd went wild. I was embarrassed that I had gotten so many.

Back then, there weren't scholarships or grants, but I received a year's subscription to *Reader's Digest*. I could join a sorority for people with high grades if I attended a university and I also got a good citizen's award.

I walked out rather dazed after it was over, expecting to stroll casually home with Mom and the neighbors when Dad came up and offered the family a ride. We actually got to ride home in his car. After arriving at home, he followed the family into the house and announced to me, "I would like to help you go to the university." I couldn't believe what I was hearing. He went on to say, "I will help you with $100." Mom was beside herself and I ran to my friends to tell them that I was going to get to go. Imagine that! Me, going to college. I was living a dream come true.

All the years of bartering and negotiating, studying and scrubbing until my knuckles were chapped all came together that night. I was going to college!

*T*rying Out Wings

I began college that fall still dressed in my flour sack peasant blouses and gathered skirts although now I spoke fluent English and wore good shoes. I was still that same tall, thin, shy girl wearing my good student halo and taking on personal challenges. Tuition wasn't yet $100 a quarter, so Dad would give me money he had promised me on graduation night a little at a time and I made up the rest by working in his shoe shop and helping my friend at her home and small bakery. She had become more than just an employer to me. I remembered the years before when some of the neighborhood children would run away, calling her a witch. I could feel her isolation even though she was careful never to allow it to show. I sensed even as a young child that she had a lonely life and I knew even from an early age that she and I would become friends. I always felt sad that I hadn't been able to see her before she passed away. She had placed herself in a nursing home by that time and I lived far away from Las Vegas, so I could not visit her often. But I never forgot her, the work ethic she taught me, and her introduction into the world of etiquette. Because of her friendship with me as a youngster and the lameness and cruelty she had to bear, she unleashed an empathy and compassion in me for those with heavy crosses to bear.

I was never embarrassed by working in the bakery, but I finally saw clearly my circumstances when the other freshmen would walk by the shoe shop and I would be inside polishing shoes, sweeping, or scrubbing. I would try to become part of the furniture, hoping they wouldn't see me and realize my deep poverty. Yet I knew the never-ending scrubbing was my only avenue toward any kind of a hopeful future, so I continued to scrub. My hands were always the same red, chapped, short-clipped hands they had been since my childhood. My hair was now short and my body was still nonexistent.

Despite my appearance, I quickly became friends with many students. They were even more friendly when some found out I was willing to read their assignments and underscore, putting questions in the margins I felt sure the professor would ask. I did so because that was the only way I had access to the books necessary for each class. My ability to continue as a student still depended on the barter system I had discovered so long ago when I traded information for crayons. Sometimes the professors would reserve the books I needed at the library for me. They were a helpful lot, wanting all the students to succeed.

One professor in particular became a very special friend. Victoria de Sánchez, in only one quarter, had shown me a different view of the world and how I felt about myself as a Hispanic woman. She didn't actually verbalize certain behaviors. She modeled them. The students in her classes would always quickly become her "hijitos" and become a close family in that particular class. I was fascinated by her way of making a point without ever verbalizing it.

I had grown up in a home where Spanish was valued and we worked hard to polish our Spanish language skills. But Hispanics at that time were conditioned to Anglicize their surnames, pronouncing them incorrectly. Victoria would repeat them in standard Spanish and continue with whatever it was she was saying. She never said anything about it, yet to this day, I know that she was making a powerful statement. It was obvious. She was proud

of her heritage. She spoke glowingly about the great things that
the Hispanic culture had contributed to our country, again, this
being a first for me to hear. Years later I would see her again
while teaching with her in Ecuador. She opened new paths for
New Mexican women both in the United States and in Latin
America and even though she is now gone, her influence is still
felt around the world.

Even though I had many friends including boys, still I had no
sweethearts. Sure, the boys liked me; they even admired me.
Many of them would dance with me, but they didn't ask me to be
their sweetheart. I was a good student and a friendly person. I
even did a lot of the campus radio shows. I loved to talk and radio
was a great solution to my painful shyness. Nobody could see me
on the radio. The drama group was called the "Koshares," but it
included a radio section. We would practice skits all week long
and then while sitting around a small round table, perform live.
I avoided drama because I would have to speak in front of people. But occasionally, I would do small parts in a Spanish play just
so I could speak my native language. I loved our radio shows even
though I never got the opportunity to perform in Spanish.

I was aware that the subtle segregation I had experienced in
grade school was still there even though at the college level one
would think it would have dissipated at least somewhat. There
were sororities I wasn't asked to join. They were filled with Anglos
and richer people. I would never have experienced belonging to a
sorority group at all if it hadn't been for one of my professors.
Even though she was Anglo and spoke very little Spanish, she was
sensitive to our culture. She was way before her time. Cultural sensitivity hadn't even become a well-known term yet. God bless her.
She saw the dilemma some of us Spanish Americans and poorer
girls were in and created a sorority solely for us. It was complete
with a secret password, candles lit for an initiation ceremony, and
even a cute little pin. She taught us about Emily Post. We
learned about meals, place settings . . . you know, all the things
the more elite kids had taken for granted since childhood but

that some of us had never been exposed to because of our poverty and skin color.

Yes, all in all, my freshman year was a happy year. I worked hard in my classes and harder yet at the shoe shop and bakery. I had set a goal in my mind of achieving an education to help my family climb out of the poverty we had been in for so long. Everything was going just as I had planned, until the day I stood in line to register for the summer session at the college. The tall, handsome young man who noticed me and struck up a conversation became my husband that first July after a whirlwind courtship.

I couldn't believe that such a handsome, sophisticated, not to mention extremely well-educated man, would take an interest in me. He had been a seminary student and along with speaking English and his native Spanish from northern New Mexico, he had also learned Latin and Greek. His opening line of conversation with me had been to read the Greek words on my sorority pin. He was brilliant and nicely mannered and for the first time in my life, I was developing a close relationship with a person who had a superb formal education. He reinforced to me how important education was. He began turning the wheels of aspiration that would continue to turn long after he was gone. He began to pull me toward a completely different world.

We left town in early September and moved to northern New Mexico. The small community where Horacio had gotten a teaching job was much more rural than Las Vegas, and my dreams of education were unwillingly put aside. Within that first year of our marriage, our first child was born. Ross quickly stole center stage in our family. Mom and Nanita spent as much time with Ross as my husband and I did. Even though Horacio taught in Canjilón (meaning "antler" in English), nearer the Colorado border, we came to Las Vegas to my mom's home whenever we could, although at first, it was a long bus ride. Later, the bus ride would turn into a long, torturous ride in the first jalopy we bought.

Canjilón was a great experience for me because of the new skills I gained while living there. My cooking skills increased tremendously and I grew to appreciate just how hard my mom had worked when she did laundry. I had to do mine the same way. The people were never strangers. I mastered the skill of making friends completely there. With the beauty of the mountains surrounding us, I grew to cherish nature and the wilderness with the same reverence my grandparents must have felt in Sapello. There was an abundance of wildflowers and arranging them quickly became a new skill.

My love of children would draw me without a conscious awareness to my husband's classroom in a one-room schoolhouse where he taught eight grades at once. The knowledge I gained from being his unpaid educational assistant was worth more than any monetary payment. Grouping, evaluation, and role playing were among the valuable lessons I learned. It was much better for the children not to be divided by age and grades. They were provided an opportunity to assume teaching, learning and sharing roles. It was a wonderful place for me to develop untried teaching methods I would later use myself as a teacher. That one-room school made me a teacher.

My grandmother, Nanita, had come to live with my mother after Grandpa had passed away. His death had been a complete shock to us all. My grandfather had always appeared strong, healthy, and completely invincible and in my twelve-year-old mind, he would be in my life forever. But while plowing one of his fields, he suffered a stroke. He must have felt ill and planned to quit for the afternoon, because he had fallen between Dick and June, the two plow horses, while trying to unhitch them near the house. Grandma had been standing on the porch and saw him fall. She ran to where he lay and struggled to move Dick and June away from him so they wouldn't inadvertently trample him under their hooves in their nervousness, sensing something was wrong. Later, she would tell me that she had yelled at all the saints to help her. Well, perhaps it was because her invocations were so loud, or because her neighbors heard her and came to help, or because one of her saints intervened on her behalf beckoning them to come, but either way, the neighbors came immediately to her assistance. Unfortunately, it was too late and Grandpa lay on that hard, dusty ground, the same ground he had taught me to love, until the coroner could come from Las Vegas several hours later. Grandma was beside herself, insisting he be moved to his bed in the house, but the neighbors wouldn't let her because the coroner would have to see him as he lay.

Grandpa's funeral was an outpouring of sympathy from friends from all walks of life. Rich and poor, young and old, Republicans and Democrats showed up for the funeral. Everybody had admired and respected Grandpa. He had touched many lives in his short sixty-two years and it seemed as though hundreds attended the rosaries and funeral. I say "rosaries," because there were two held. His very dear friend and my mother's second cousin, Lieutenant Governor Ceferino Quintana, could not come until a day later, so a rosary was recited two nights in a row, giving him time to get to town. People packed the church both nights, and when everyone had settled down, the Sociedad de San Antonio, represented by about twelve men, proceeded up the aisle to the front of the church. They knelt in front of Grandpa's coffin, and the next hour was spent listening, reciting, and praying. Rosaries could be heard clinking against the pew backs when someone would shift position to ease knees falling asleep and someone's sniffles would occasionally break through my concentration on the beautiful and comforting words being said.

Catholic Latinos attend many rosaries and funerals throughout their lifetime because these are part of a deeply ingrained tradition. It had been no different for me; I had attended dozens. But Grandpa's will always remain clearly fixed in my mind. Years later, every time I would walk up the steps of a stage to speak on human rights, I would think of my viejito and say, "This one's for you, Grandpa. I know you're watching me and are proud of your shy, withdrawn hijita sharing the beliefs you taught me." And with that thought, I could just feel his large, deeply tanned, strong arms wrap around me in one of his famous abrazos, giving me the strength I needed to begin speaking to the audience.

Grandma and Grandpa's farm in Sapello was on a government loan, and Grandma lost almost everything when Grandpa died. Although my sister helped with the loan, Grandma agreed to move in with us. She no longer wanted to be alone at the ranch. So when Ross, our first child, was born, he was pampered by Mom and Grandma for many years. His curly, dark-colored hair and rosy cheeks were similar to my brother's when he was a child. His quick mind was a joy to see. Many times I would be in Mom's tiny little kitchen baking a pie or cake and could hear their laughter from the other room.

Our favorite outfit for him as a baby was a yellow jacket and pants, like the colors of a parrot. People would say words to him and at the age of ten months, he would say them right back. He was just like a perico, which is maybe why when he reached first grade, he was already reading at the fourth-grade level.

When Rick, our second son, was born exactly three years and seven hours later than our first one, we had moved back to Las Vegas from another small rural community near Canjilón called Cebolla (onion). Rick was just as verbal as Ross and just as precocious. He was a little darker, with straight hair more like mine and the roundest eyes that would fool one into thinking of him as a santito. We learned quickly though that the term "small saint" was not created for Rick. With the two of them around, a day never went by that la familia wasn't in stitches laughing or in panic from their current antics. One day when Ross was seven, he decided that he was going to be a weight lifter. So over his head went a rather long metal bar. Still the imitator, Rick had to do the same as his big brother, but the bar was too heavy and he dropped it on his head. I remember Ross calling out in panic, "Mom! Mom! Rick hurt himself!" Off we went to the doctor. Luckily, Rick was not hurt, but I never forgot that day, which must have been like the day my mother experienced with my sister on Hermit's Peak.

The most important asset of my life up to that point was the desire of mi familia that I achieve my goal of an education. There's a lot to be said for the close-knit tightness of la familia. I could go to the library and study because I knew that when I got home my children would be there with my family. Mom and Grandma supported and encouraged me to finish my degree. They wanted me to have what they could never have dared to dream of for themselves. My husband encouraged me too. His education had been his way out of poverty also. Our family grew by one more, finally a girl this time, when I was almost finished with my B.A. in education. Carla was a mop of curls. She was neither light nor dark and definitely in a class all her own. The boys would coerce her into being their partner in pranks and Carla would always give it her best. Unlike the halo I wore as a child, Carla's was a little lopsided. Mom, Nanita, and I would send our beautiful hijita to school in the morning dressed like a china doll, but by the time she would get home in the afternoon, there was no resemblance to our angel left. The ruffles that decorated her panties would be ripped off from going down the slide too many times and her once cute little dress would be a dingy shade of brown. To top it all off, I could never imagine anyone being louder than my two boys, but Carla could squeal louder than the two of them put together. Every day she would inform me, "Mom, Mom, the boys are copying me." It may not seem like a big deal to an adult, but to Carla it was the end of the world. She would constantly yell at Ross and Rick, "Boys, leave me alone!" They would just laugh. Ah, the life of a girl with only brothers to play with.

When I had only one semester left to go, the parachute factory I had been working in to earn money for the family and my education closed and I couldn't afford university classes. I had hoped to save the money so I could go the next semester, but I didn't really feel in my heart that I would be able to finish my education for a long time. The only positive thing about the closure of the factory was that the bruises on my back finally went away. I was still so thin, weighing in at 114 pounds, that every vertebra had a black bruise on it from pulling tons of parachute material through the sewing machine while using the hard back of the chair for support.

While wondering if I would ever finish, the same teacher that had tried to convince me I was Syrian when I was in high school came to see me one day. Nell Doherty, who had become more than just a teacher to me, said she had recently heard I was no longer in school. I told her about the factory closing and my hopes to save money and go back in the future. She said, "No, Mari-Luci, if you put it off another semester, you won't finish. I'm going to lend you the money so you can go to school this semester."

I said, "No, I can't accept it. What if I can't pay it back?" I panicked at the thought that she was going to lend me money.

She replied, "I'll tell you what. We'll make a deal. Although I'm lending the money to you, if you can't pay it back, then some day when you're out in the world earning money, you give the same chance I'm giving you to another student."

I thought about it for only an instant. I could do that. If I couldn't pay her, I could help students down the road accomplish their dream of a good education and a better life. I said, "Yes!" She gave me three hundred dollars standing right there in my driveway.

When I wanted to give her an IOU, she said, "No. We are friends." Neither of us had any idea at the time what kind of seed had been planted that day. I would think of her years later when I was able to keep my promise many times over. I have helped dozens of students in a variety of ways to earn their degrees.

So with that three hundred dollars, I went to school, bought all the books I needed my last semester, and graduated from college with a teaching degree. That was in December. In January of 1956, I got my first teaching job and started saving money until I had the correct amount and took it to my teacher and friend and said, "Here's your money, but I'm still going to live up to the other half of the deal."

So finally, almost nine years after starting my university education, I received my diploma. I didn't give up on it, ever. While achieving this personal goal, Mom and Nanita ended up playing the traditional Spanish role in which the entire family helps in the upbringing of all the children. They had taken care of "mis tres changuitos" while I was in classes during the day. My husband would help them with the kids at night so I could study. Over those long nine years, I felt as if I had walked a thousand miles back and forth after work to the university with my pile of books. All was well though, because I knew my three kids were at home, safe and sound and well cared for. My education had really been a family enterprise.

With two paychecks, small as they were, my husband and I started becoming an upwardly mobile family. Horacio's and my teaching jobs enabled us to afford activities such as Cub Scouts and Brownies for our kids. They had every extracurricular activity we could possibly think of. Art, music, and dance lessons were a must. All the things that would help our children get a well-rounded education became a priority. La familia wanted to guarantee that this generation would not suffer the pains of poverty we had endured. Even my sister, Elvira, continued to help long distance. She had moved to California long ago, but always sent money, clothes, or educational toys to help.

We had been able to replace our first vehicle with one that stayed together with more than string and rubber bands. It was a good thing since I was going in three directions as a chauffeur every day. Our first "junker," which had only cardboard as a window on the passenger side, was hardly reliable. I would have to pull that worn piece of cardboard down to tell my husband if cars were coming from the other direction, even if it was a cold, wet, and rainy day. My husband taught me how to drive "Beulah," as we had fondly dubbed that ugly car. Despite its homeliness, I have always had a special place for it in my heart.

The teaching position I was fortunate enough to get was in a small community south of Las Vegas on top of a mesa. My husband taught at the bottom of the mesa in another small community. He had bought a pair of axles with the wheels attached and added a wood floor, walls, and a roof, and it became a tiny mobile home. We moved it from Las Vegas. With the addition of a small couch and cookstove, but no indoor toilet or water, it became our apartment during the week. We would go back to Las Vegas on the weekends to see la familia and our children who stayed with my mom and Nanita so they could attend school there.

I thought younger children were the ideal age to teach because my student teaching was in the second grade. I loved to work with children of that age. But my first teaching position was a combination classroom of third, fourth, and fifth grades. The students had run off two substitute teachers in the first semester so I knew I was in for it when I arrived. But luckily for me, with my natural ability to make friends, I quickly identified the troublemakers and became friends with them. I was very happy working there that semester.

I learned so much. I adapted some of the techniques I had learned in Canjilón. Now I knew how to turn behavior problem children into leaders. I got parents that weren't involved to acknowledge what their children were doing. I worked very hard at trying to befriend the parents and other teachers. Along with this, I learned from the children themselves.

We had a small potbellied stove that stood in the middle of our classroom for heat. One day while I had a group of children in a corner for reading and the rest of the class was working on an assignment, one young man decided to beef up the fire. He shoved a whole lot of logs into that poor old stove when I wasn't looking. It didn't take long before the children began to complain about the heat. When I looked up to see what the disturbance was, I saw the little stove. It had turned almost completely red, its belly looking like a red tomato. I opened all the windows and quickly lined up the children and took them outside to look for, of all things, signs of spring.

The other two teachers housed in the building probably wondered what the heck we were doing, dashing out of the classroom on that cold, wintry day. But the classroom had become unbearably warm, so off we had gone on our field trip through the sandy mesas looking for our signs of spring. I don't even remember if we found any, but twenty minutes later when I took the children back, the stove had changed back to black, the classroom was not nearly so warm, and I had learned my lesson.

I created a new position and turned the troublemaker into the stove monitor. From then on, he had to keep the room temperature according to the thermometer I hung on the wall and keep records on a chart. With that solution, we were able to eliminate further wintry field trips.

Not long afterwards, I was on playground duty. I enjoyed it immensely because I could teach the children new games. But this particular day, as we were going around in a circle, all of a sudden the children squatted down and put their heads between their legs. I was the only one left standing. Baffled by their odd behavior, I began to question them, opening my mouth to say, "What's the matter?" and a gust of sand hit me. The children were conditioned to know when the wind would come blowing in on the mesa, making the sand fly something terrible. It was like a sixth sense. They could feel or hear it coming and prepare for it. I didn't know you were supposed to do that. That sand caught me completely unawares. When I heard the sound right next to me, I turned to face it and all the sand got in my mouth, my eyes, and my hair. It was ghastly but over in a flash. The kids instantly got up to play, but I couldn't continue. I hadn't squatted down. In fact, I hadn't even kept my mouth closed. I was the sorriest sight you ever saw. My face was white with sand. My hair stood straight up. I had to leave the children to play alone while I made an attempt to clean myself up and be presentable by the time class started again. It took several days to completely rid myself of the minuscule granules.

During the next two years I worked my way back to Las Vegas. I had taught kindergarten through fifth grade and in those two years had gained a lot of teaching experience. Las Vegas was growing, which resulted in some large classes. Little did I know that would become my big break. Because of the size of my class, the university would send prospective teachers to observe me. They liked what I was doing, so before long, I had one or two student teachers every semester. The supervising professor who happened to be the chairman of the Education Department at the university would come to observe the student teachers in my classroom and ended up inviting me to teach during the summers at Highlands. So began my college career as a professor, even though I only had a master's degree. Almost all universities require a Ph.D. to teach there.

After several years of teaching, the superintendent asked me to start a remedial reading program because I had taught the course at Highlands University the previous summer. So I set up the first remedial reading program in the west Las Vegas school system. I traveled to three different schools and taught remedial reading to small groups.

I was full of energy and so eager to help children get their education. After much testing of students and setting up a magnificent area behind the principal's office, I was ready to begin my first day. My first group was two third-grade boys. They came in and I did all the things I had done with others in remedial reading to make them feel at home. I showed them all the things we would be working with. I went on and on, hoping to make my first two boys feel very secure in a brand new ambiance. I was almost ready to begin the actual lesson with them when I said, "Now, from what I understand, you're having a little bit of trouble with reading."

One of the boys, the tinier of the two said, "Oh, no, ma'am, we don't have trouble with the reading, we just have trouble with the words." In their innocence, they put me in my proper place. There are always ways children make us adults feel humble and keep our superior knowledge and experience from going to our heads.

By my last year in Las Vegas three years later, I had become the language arts supervisor for the entire county system. It covered a radius of eighty miles. I advised teachers, demonstrating to them how to work with students with reading problems. By then, I had spent eight years in the education loop.

My husband's new job at the University of New Mexico (UNM) in Albuquerque in 1964 forced us to break with Las Vegas, but not with mi familia. My mother and grandmother were still a vital part of our family even though they stayed in Las Vegas. I chose to teach in a barrio school. I had gone the previous summer to a language institute at UCLA. I was using the latest techniques in methodology in English as a second language. I enjoyed my time there very much and word of my expertise spread. By the end of three months, the dean of the College of Education at UNM had invited me to join the faculty at the university and teach English as a second language with the same techniques I used with children, to Latin American students who were coming to campus for a special project. These adults would take their classes in Spanish but needed conversational English. That's where I would come in.

I wanted so badly to accept this new challenge but was scared of giving up the secure job that I desperately needed at that time. My principal finally told me, "I'll tell you what. I won't hire a permanent substitute teacher for you yet. You try it out for a while and if you don't like it, you can come back. Your job will still be here." With that possibility, I accepted the new position.

Within the first week I called him, saying, "I love my job. The adults' eyes light up when they understand, just like kids'." I was now officially working at UNM without credentials, in a basement office, and by the end of my first year, I had grown from English as a second language classes to full-blown university courses, teaching the Latino students in Spanish. I was in the right place at the right time. There were few Spanish-speaking professors for this special project. Most of us Spanish-speakers were still struggling in the trenches because of the poverty levels that hindered us from further education.

I think being a successful teacher was just part of my nature. It had always been my way to help people with less than myself any way I could. I would see those youngsters in front of me desperately needing help and I would kick into gear. The suffering I had seen as a child when there was no social promotion and the humiliation those bigger boys endured stayed with me. I was determined that all my many children would always move ahead smartly because they would know everything there was to know. I believed education could get anyone out of poverty and I intended to do everything I could every day to help those children and young adults.

Those days were a blessing of ignorance. My ideals were still innocent. I had not gained the experience I would receive many years later that would show me just how naive my ideals were. Education alone wouldn't be enough. A person could have as many degrees as a thermometer, but without the "right" skin color, he or she could still remain at poverty level if others so chose.

My classroom was my favorite place to be. It was fun for me to see everyone working at top speed, accumulating knowledge that would help improve their quality of life. All my experiences of childhood, added to the wonderful professors who had prepared me so successfully for my teaching career, had made it the only logical choice for me. I hadn't really had a driving desire to become a teacher when I started college; it just happened, mostly because teaching was the only thing available. But now I knew I had been groomed for it since my earliest memories.

My Latino students reinforced all my own beliefs and the way of life my parents had taught me. My language and culture were beginning to be indisputably validated. They had vocabulary I didn't know but quickly learned from each different Latin American country. It was the first time I had used my Spanish with individuals who truly respected it. It was not considered the language of the poor. These students were professionals in their countries. They were proud of their cultures and their countries and wanted to share their ways of life and language with Americans.

I thrived on this new experience. I loved the feeling of equality. No longer was I just a poor shoemaker's daughter who didn't know when to raise her hand in class. I was a professional sharing with other professionals in a language and an understanding of culture that many could not begin to comprehend. I had never needed much sleep to be revitalized for each day, but now I was so excited that I rarely slept at all. There were so many positive things happening in my professional life that were reinforcing who I was and where I came from that I didn't fully internalize the signs of downslide in my personal life.

chapter

A Blessing in Disguise

"You gotta help, you gotta help!" sounded my battle cry. I was leaning against my pulpit, my knees knocking together loudly, I might add, where hopefully no one could hear them. The podium I was currently hiding behind had, on many occasions, become my best friend. I was scared stiff and my knuckles were white because they were clasped onto the sides of my friend so tightly. But I was up there and I had something important to say. "Society can open up and help people so they will not be trapped in their given circumstances. Society can help to find ways out!" After all, I was living proof. I ate tortillas in public now. I didn't hide them in my brown lunch bag anymore as I had done in high school. Someone, somewhere, had helped me push forward.

Sometimes, like tonight, when I was speaking to a particularly uncooperative crowd, I would wonder just why I had accepted this new job at the university. A large civil rights project had been awarded to the university and when I had been asked to join the team on the project, I had emphatically said, "Yes!" Fighting for the underdog had always been my personal campaign, but now I could be heard on a national level. I really wanted to continue to help the poor in more visible ways.

But it took a lot of thinking before changing jobs. I was having so much fun traveling to Central and South America supervising or teaching. I knew I was helping relations between our respective countries and assisting our students tremendously. There was so much I hadn't known about myself before that I now realized. I had discovered that one of my passions was to travel and meet new people and it had become clear to me that I really had become a strong voice for the forgotten. Even though still very scared, I could speak in defense of those who had the smallest voices but needed the most help, the poor and the minorities. Having had no adventures in my childhood, travel and meeting new people had become an endorphin. So, while this new opportunity working in civil rights still included traveling, it was limited to the continental United States. It was not as exciting and adventuresome as traveling abroad, but more important, it was an opportunity to further my deeply felt personal cause.

Eventually, this decision would guide my journey on a path that would lead me into becoming a vice president at the University of New Mexico. My personal agenda included trying to help recruit minority professors into the tenure track. When minority professors were hired on soft funds, their positions disappeared when the outside funding was no longer available. I saw wonderful professors come and go. I wanted to help attract the best, but on hard funds so that they would become part of the system. In this manner, they could help influence policy that affected students. I wanted minority students to feel extra welcome and hugely successful at the university.

I was beginning to find out that the best way to help people was through influencing policies. The changes one fights for stay with the system a little longer. For now, I was a civil rights worker addressing and challenging large groups all over the nation to make changes in how they viewed and serviced minority students. And that was why my knees were quaking and my nails were marring the wood of the podium on this particular night. Sheer fright!

Our small team of civil rights workers was diverse. We all had our specialty and areas of expertise. One person on our team was a statistician. While he could give us ammunition such as statistics that showed a close to 50 percent Hispanic dropout rate in high schools across the nation, he was an Anglo and didn't have some of the personal insight that the rest of us had. But that didn't inhibit his tenacity. He fed us the important information.

Another team member was a fellow Las Vegan. We had known each other since high school days and the university. He always made sure I got safely to my hotel room at nights after our seminars and would almost always meet me early in the morning to start preparations for the next day's workshop. He was a counselor and a teacher. We were good friends.

Two other members had been professors and close friends at the University of New Mexico, and other educators who later joined us had been raised in small towns in northern New Mexico. For a long time, I was the only woman on the team, and usually my boss and I were the ones standing in front of the crowd doing most of the talking. Ironically enough, we all had a background in education with the exception of one member.

I would stand there on the platform, usually in a conservative business suit and high heels suitable for a woman who was meant to be taken seriously, using every ideology and paradigm I knew in an attempt to get my audience to begin to understand or at least agree with the concepts I was trying to share with them. Icebreakers were a standard activity used at the beginning of most of our workshops. Lemons would be put in a basket and everyone in the room had to take one. The participants were asked to examine theirs closely for identifying marks. Then the basket would be passed and all the fruit put back in. The participants were then asked to find their particular lemon. Almost everyone always could, and at the end of their comments of surprise at being able to do so, we would liken the lemons to children and say, "If you look at kids, how individual they must be if even a lemon could be that different to be found in a basket of many."

Even working exceptionally hard in preparing my remarks, and improving them after each presentation, sometimes I still would not reach the entire audience. Counting how many folded arms were in the crowd had evolved into a fun ritual for our group. One of us would stand offstage while another was speaking and literally count the folded arms.

When we were speaking we could tell if we were reaching our audience by noticing whether people were tapping the shoulders of the people in front of them or whispering in their ears. Notes written on slips of paper would be passed around and an undercurrent of consistent rustling could be heard from the wiggling and shuffling of the audience. It could be likened to teaching students something they weren't interested in or didn't care about and trying to get them to pay attention to your lesson. Only these weren't young students, this wasn't a classroom, and you couldn't call their parents!

Most individuals in education—principals, teachers, secretaries, and even the janitors—work hard to reach kids. But in the groups we addressed, there was always an element of fidgeting teachers, principals, superintendents, and many others who were harder to reach than the toughest kid. Some of them would sit in a position that said, "I dare you to teach me anything." The teachers weren't concerned with including the parents of minority students in their children's education. They couldn't be bothered to include a holiday or special game or dance that belonged to the quiet ones that didn't speak up in class. It didn't occur to them that these quiet ones might not know how to speak English as well as another language. I knew that one from experience. First grade wasn't easy for me in the beginning, either. They believed the stereotypes that clung to the students who were darker skinned or whose clothes weren't as new as the other children's.

On one occasion as I was preparing for the next day's workshop with the superintendent of a neighboring school district, I innocently asked, "How many students do you have?"

He turned to me and asked in his blissful ignorance, "Counting the Mexicans?" It was obvious he had two counts in his head. I had just said "students." He had distinguished two classes between the students . . . richer, poorer . . . lighter, darker . . . English-speaking, Spanish-speaking. The United States was supposed to be classless, yet here a class system was being taught to the children by the examples demonstrated by many of their own teachers and principals.

This new job of mine, because I wanted to make a difference so badly, forced me into the exposure of speaking in public more and more. My boss insisted I tell audiences the things I would tell him in the office. I spoke at seminars and workshops. I asked people around the country to be aware of individual cultures. "Be aware of how we learn and accept us for who we are," I would repeat over and over. School districts around the nation asked for our assistance in helping to desegregate their schools, not by choice, but by federal mandate. We would try to help sensitize them. We would ask them what kinds of things they could do to better reach the Spanish or Mexican American child, the Native American child, or the Black child. We would ask them to involve parents and to remember that children have individual needs because all peoples are culturally bound.

My insight was partly due to the unique state I grew up in. There were reservations throughout the state. Northern New Mexico where I had grown up was rather separated from the rest of the state and had kept much of its original Spanish flavor. Southern New Mexico bordered Mexico and had experienced an influx of Mexican culture. With the variety of these various cultures plus the influx of Anglo groups transferring to the state, New Mexico didn't seem to have the horrendous racial problems found in other states. Since New Mexico missed much of the more severe racial separation found in the other states, people concentrated their efforts to ensure cultural sensitivity. Ongoing training and awareness workshops were held for educators, boards of education, and superintendents so they would become aware of problems and wage war by influencing curricula to include cultural sensitivity. It was natural that the University of New Mexico would receive an important project such as ours. We already appeared to be years ahead of other parts of the country.

While New Mexico was definitely touched by the civil rights movement, beyond its borders, the rest of the country was in a much bigger spin. The myth that the United States had no social classes was being challenged. People grew up being taught to believe that they were all alike and that anyone could aspire to be president of the country. Yet many of us knew that in real life, there were social classes that affected individuals. It was being shouted from the rooftops to the streets below, from college campuses to middle-class suburbs that it was no longer OK for people to not have the basic necessities of life. Everyone should have a home, everyone should receive an equal education, everyone qualified for a job should get the opportunity, everyone deserved a chance. People were beginning to speak out about the cruel conditions under which they lived.

My shyness from youth had never left me, but now I was speaking and challenging people to change. "Accept the fact that not everyone is alike. Spanish and Mexican Americans are equal to everyone else and deserve to be acknowledged. Their ways are beautiful and should not be lost in the mainstream," I would preach. My attempts to influence policies around the country concerning minorities and low-income people taught me quickly that it's not human nature to warm to the idea of behavioral modification, especially when a Mexican American first-grade female school teacher is the one challenging you to do so.

Occasionally, the racist groups or individuals in the crowd I was addressing would become very difficult for me to face and even get downright insolent. So on this particular night while I was on the stage, gripping the podium as if my very life depended on it, trumpeting my battle cry, the plane at the small airport had its engines running, ready to whisk me away at the first sign of trouble. The superintendent hadn't told me before my speech, but there had been a death threat against the outside Mexican agitator—me. They weren't taking any chances. The police were there along with a squad car to whisk me to my getaway plane if it became necessary and I needed to make a run for it. I didn't know this was going on beforehand, so I was at ease, encouraging everyone I possibly could to open up the system for more opportunities for minorities.

Even though I was often petrified, I was telling university presidents and superintendents that terrible things were happening to our students in the classrooms. Often there was much we could do to alleviate the problems. All teachers and professors had to be sensitized so they would understand. Not only did I preach it, but I would give examples. In classrooms I would demonstrate lessons showing special sensitivity to minorities. I was never afraid of that. I was a schoolteacher and loved to be with children whether they were rich or poor; brown, black or white; in my country or in Latin America.

Following my religious convictions, which had taught me that everyone was God's own design and had a specific job to do while on earth, I became convinced that my mission here was to help the poor in whatever way I could. "The poorest of the poor," I would keep saying. "There but for the grace of God go I. You gotta help, you gotta help." That became my way of life and my guiding principle in whatever I did. My civil rights work had changed me, opening my eyes to the rest of the country and its temperaments. I had finally made a very public stand and was doing something about the problems, something I felt I had been groomed for since I was a child. I had come into my own. I finally realized who I was and what I was about. And so that's how it also happened that after twenty-one years of marriage, I thought about and got a divorce.

My divorce during my civil rights work almost devastated me. I was being torn between what I had been raised to be and what I had grown up to become. Not realizing it at the time, my divorce was a catalyst that moved me toward the discovery of what my fight for human rights really would become, which would be even more intense that what I was now feeling.

I had been taught as a young girl by my mother's example that women should endure all their husbands' behaviors, habits, and values. Marriage could end up being the cross you had to bear in life, but there was no choice in the matter. If you were married, you just gritted your teeth and bore it. Sacred unions weren't always like the fairy tale about Cinderella we read and fantasized about as children and teenagers. Not all men could be handsome princes and—especially for Catholics—there was little room for a marriage to dissolve.

So since I was Catholic and saw my mother carry her cross so quietly for so many years, accepting without questioning, I went into a major slump when I finally decided to face the truth that my marriage wasn't working. Mom had loved Dad until she died. Despite what he had put our family through, Mom never had a mean thing to say about him. She would always remind us that he was our dad. So when there had been no way to hold my marriage together after it had broken apart completely and after seeing my mom endure for so many years, I felt like a complete failure. There were serious problems in my marriage that I no longer wanted to tolerate.

But I still wondered if there had been something more I could have done to save our marriage. I had lived in my husband's shadow since I was eighteen and admired him greatly. He was a brilliant man and had earned a Ph.D., one of the first Hispanics to earn one in educational administration. He was conducting research and writing exciting articles. With my decision to divorce, I felt ripped right down the middle. My new enlightened side said, "I can still retain my beliefs and do this!" My traditional side argued that there was no room for a divorce. My shy side reminded me, "Who are you? You just happened to be in the right place at the right time and were given the opportunity to teach at the university level." I was middle-aged, still as gangly looking and as shy as ever, and nothing more than a simple school teacher. What was I to do with my life now?

But my fortune came in the form of the many friends I had. I had no idea there were so many people in my corner. It was they who came to my rescue. Janitors, secretaries, coworkers, students—you name it—they helped me through. "No, no, Mari-Luci," they would say. "Don't stay at home. You come to school and work on a degree."

I would argue with them, saying, "I can't possibly do that, I'm a first-grade teacher."

They would insist, "You can!" They'd see me with tears in my eyes and take me to the student union building and drown me in coffee, picking and pulling me up. They were wonderful. I was blessed. My empathy and encouragement of others to be their best came back to me in my time of need tenfold.

So since all three of my children were now grown up and in college themselves, I took my friends' advice, rolled up my shirtsleeves, and dug in to further my own education. It was my way back out of the uninteresting black hole that had become my life. It was the driving force that kept me from thinking about my failed marriage. My mother's words echoed in my ear: "Education is the way out of poverty." My friends pushed and tugged to get me through. I achieved what I thought was unobtainable for the poor daughter of a shoemaker—a Ph.D.

I admit there were moments when I felt so alone that it was hard to keep the studies going. I thought my children would continue their college careers close to home, but one by one, they all left for other colleges . . . other states . . . other lives. I asked my mom and Nanita to come and live with me in Albuquerque to fill the big void I was feeling. But while Nanita would have come, Mom wasn't ready to give up her own home at that stage in her life. She had finally shaken off the chains of authority inflicted upon her since her marriage and no amount of coaxing on my part and trying to sway her decision could persuade her to move. I was totally physically alone for the first time in my life. But because I was so involved with my students, and my colleagues were so nice, I was able to get over that unwelcome hump too.

I was finally having a great time furthering my education until two semesters before I was to finish my degree. I had really had no serious roadblocks until a university administrator read me the fine print in the university catalog stating, "You cannot work full-time at the university and be a full-time graduate student." That was exactly what I was doing. But I couldn't let up, not now. So I worked around the fine print. I continued working as a full-time student with my full-time job in the civil rights project. I just accepted half the pay for my twelve- to fourteen-hour days. Although I was promised that my job would let up a little, it never did. I continued speaking at seminars or keynoting at conferences all across the nation. I was constantly going places. Too bad frequent flyer programs were not common then. My reputation as a speaker had grown nationally, and my boss felt I had to honor every invitation that appeared. Because I slept little, I was able to keep my head above water. I never felt tired; I loved how I earned my living.

I had to do all that for a year. It was difficult because I was helping my children financially at their universities and helping support my mom and grandmother, but somehow I survived. At the age of forty-three, in 1971, I received my doctorate with a major in curriculum and instruction and a minor in Latin American studies.

After earning my degree, I kept my same job, enjoying every minute of it. People would ask me all the time, "Why did you get a degree if you're going to keep the same job?"

I would answer, "I only needed a degree because it got me out of the rut I was in when I was so low after the divorce." I never saw it as a passport to move on to something else. I was perfectly happy with what I was doing. I had no idea that what I used to think of as the end of my life when I got divorced would end up being the beginning.

With that Ph.D., I began teaching many more courses, writing, and doing even more community service. Within seven years, I went from assistant professor to an associate professor and onto full professor. Normally that last rung on the climb up the career ladder happens toward the end of one's teaching career, but then, I hardly considered myself among the norm. My guardian angel loved me. I ended my "teaching" career as associate dean in the College of Education. I didn't know it then, but I would never have time to go back into teaching because of my future involvement in professional administration and policy making. People had always commented on my uncanny ability to get into other people's shoes and feel what they were feeling. My success in reaching the toughest skeptic was in the empathy I had found hidden inside myself as a child. My eyes would always tear up with their compliments. I would reply, "It feels right to help people. I love doing it." I didn't realize until now, when professionals would come up to tell me I had taught them to read in second grade, that I had left a trail full of vigorous signs that I was having a positive effect on the people I was trying to help.

I began to fantasize that perhaps I could really make a difference in some people's lives. I would have to work at it very hard, but maybe I could make a lasting difference. I wanted to help everyone get out of poverty through education. People often tried to pay me for helping them. I would say in reply, "I have a talent that God has given me. I understand people. I ask nothing for myself, but you can pay me back by helping somebody else that needs helping. It can be monetary. It can be lending an ear. It can be whatever you want, whatever fits your style. But go out and do something for others." I was returning the favor bestowed on me those many years before by my teacher, tenfold. If only she had lived to see her seed of goodwill germinate in so many places.

So believing in what seemed like an impossible dream, I had dared to step into the spotlight and challenge the league of educators to do everything they could to help minority students. "Don't just find room in your heart to help those people that no one pays attention to, but help change activities, attitudes, and policy! It doesn't have to be dramatic changes. Consider hiring a bilingual individual that speaks Spanish the next time you have an employee opening. We will help you find people with the right qualifications. Perhaps you could set a goal that rather than just ESL students learning a second language, English, all the children could learn a second language. It doesn't have to be Spanish, either. It could be French, German, or something else. ESL programs could be aggressively expanded into high schools rather than almost dropped completely at the elementary school level." I never ran out of easily implemented ideas and suggestions on how to help students feel equal and feel their culture validated.

My work was not easy because I had to write all my speeches. I was not an extemporaneous speaker. My words were from my heart, my soul, and my roots and no one else could possibly understand and say what was inside of me waiting to get out and be announced. I couldn't stand in front of a crowd without the security of my paper and my podium. I wrote papers like crazy. Pamphlets also. If the College of Education secretary couldn't get to it, I did it by hand with pencil and yellow tablet paper. My pace was driven relentlessly from my very depths. But I had seen a change, not only in myself since my divorce, but in many school districts around me. Our trumpet had been sounded in major cities such as New York, Chicago, and Los Angeles and many educators and other leaders were listening.

The changes weren't dramatic, but people were becoming aware. They were talking about things no one had talked about before. They talked about Hispanic dropout rates. They were realizing that Spanish and Mexican American kids were having many problems in schools. It was finally coming out into the open. Monolingual English teachers began making efforts to learn Spanish. They didn't expect to converse like native Spanish speakers, but they were motivated to communicate to their students in their native language. Many more school and community plays were done in Spanish. Mariachi music could be heard everywhere. It was quite a difference in a nation that several years before had not seen tortillas in school cafeterias.

My civil rights days were quite difficult. Many people think that the civil rights movement was tough only for Blacks. They don't realize how much Hispanics suffered. The majority of Hispanics were neither white nor black; they were brown. They were somewhere in between, so a very special case had to be made for them. Many people thought they just needed to get jobs and work and everything would be fine. But because Hispanics were physically identifiable, many were left out of opportunities for high-quality education and high-paying jobs. Where an entire culture of people could have been educated to improve their circumstances in each successive generation, only a few had been able to escape from their limitations as I had. The majority remained poor and vastly undereducated.

It was a consciousness-raising time for the Hispanics who had been left out of the opportunity structure in our nation. It was also a realization for me. I had been raised to believe that education was all one needed to crawl out of the bottomless well of poverty. My civil rights work had taught me that it wasn't so. Skin color could influence how a teacher would react and behave toward you. Expectations could be very different for Hispanics. Children could be treated as though they weren't very smart and as a result, their aspirations as adults were, not surprisingly, low.

What I didn't realize at the time was that I was doing something else. I was also calling attention to myself, making a name for myself in places I would never have dreamed of. Little did I know that I had been grooming myself for my next job, and little did I imagine that I would someday remarry.

I had been asked for my hand in marriage by a Colombian man who had come to the United States as a student working on his Ph.D. He had asked me to go out with him and I had accepted. It was the first time he asked me to dance that I got hooked. His movements were so different than my grandfather's had been. He moved as if he were the notes bouncing up and down on a sheet of music. His hips swayed and his knees bent and he would swing me around and around until the worries and battles in my world were just a blur outside my vision.

He was taller than I was and muscular with very broad shoulders. Broad enough, I thought, to share the responsibility of being the spouse of a fighter for minorities such as I had become. His hair was curly and brown and his eyes were always animated. But most importantly, he danced divinely. We would go dancing often, and I would float on a cloud in his arms while we moved across the dance floor. I had finally found a dance partner and "The Blue Danube" in Germany and Latino music in Casa Blanca and the rest of Morocco would become the symphony that followed me up to the heavens where he would carry me. We danced our way across Latin America and Europe.

His manners were impeccable. He was a Latino, a lover of life, a man who appreciated the inner beauty of a person as much as the outer beauty. He was sophisticated and always knew just what to say. His consideration of me was tremendous. I had hoped but had not dared to think that this man would envision a union between us. An emerald ring sealed the deal and I realized I needed to tell my family, but mostly my mom.

Though it sounds as though I had found that fantasy that my friends and I had giggled over as children, which included a castle and a handsome prince on a galloping white stallion, this marriage was a serious step for me. I was still Catholic and Catholics couldn't remarry—or divorce. When I talked with my mom, she said, "Hijita, if you had been meant to be a single person and join the nunnery, it would be different. But you really wanted to get married and have a family. You've had a hard life. I'm very happy for you that you're remarrying." Mom would have never used the nuns as an example if she had realized how captivated I was with the nuns at the Catholic school so very long ago. I had never told her how fascinated I had been by them.

Looking back, I realize now that my mother was telling me not to repeat the mistake she had made. Even though she loved my dad till the end, she wished her life had been different. I was being given a chance to do what Mom hadn't done. So, with her blessing, I remarried, taking along with me my still old-fashioned ideals by accepting his last name as my own rather than keeping my maiden name as other professional women had begun to do.

What had seemed like the end of my life a few years before had really been the beginning. I was fulfilling the driving need in myself to fight for human rights. I was also making an attempt at personal happiness. My insight didn't alert me to the future in store for me and just when I thought my life was on the road God had wanted me to travel, I would find out I had just begun to fight.

Who, Me?

I stifled the sigh that was beginning to form in my throat as my eye caught the *viejo* staring at me from his place on the wall. It was a pencil etching of a very old Chicano farmer. His face was lined with years of exposure to the hot desert sun while toiling in his fields. His hands clearly showed the abuse of hard work, and his clothing was faded and bore the signs of constant use. It was clear that as hard as he struggled, he barely earned a living. His hands rested on a century-old adobe wall and you knew his small adobe house with the rusted tin roof was just out of sight.

The Chicano and the wall seemed to be one . . . motionless in time, yet vibrant with a rich history. Everyone who came into my office always commented about that etching. I would quickly volunteer, "That viejo keeps me honest. Every time I think it would be easier to pretend I am not aware of what transpires with Chicano students, I look at him and know I must write that memo or make that telephone call . . . regardless of how much trouble it's going to be for me. Or every time a recent title or award is going to my head, I look at him. That old man is my conscience." And that conscience was now reminding me that even though I was finishing preparations for next week's classes so I wouldn't have to take work home over the weekend for a change, I should answer the ringing phone. "You never know who could be calling."

Suppressing my sigh, I picked up the phone, saying, "Hello, this is Mari-Luci." A female voice responded, telling me to wait for a person from the Department of State. That's odd, I thought. I wondered who it could be. Most of my calls from Washington were from the Department of Health, Education, and Welfare. Waiting for further enlightenment, the two pictures hanging next to the old man caught my attention. They were both of children playing. I guess subconsciously I had tried to show the breadth of what we described to our bicultural classes at the university as "Hispanic" culture. *La Piñata* was a Venezuelan painting of children playing on a beautiful, warm April day, just like today. They were attempting to crack open a piñata with a stick. A little boy, who at the moment had the coveted stick, was blindfolded, of course, to make the game both more fun and more difficult. He was in the middle of his swing. To the side was an adult pulling on a rope attached to the piñata to keep it constantly in motion and make the game last until the children could hardly stand the anticipation of diving in on the treats freed from their confines. One could only speculate as to whether the boy would be the lucky one to split open the piñata. You could almost hear the laughter spilling out of the painting as the children shouted their directions for where he should swing his stick.

The other picture was from Ecuador. These children were playing instruments native to their country. The dancing and singing and movement of the picture always energized me. Dancing was the means by which I could enjoy the music I had yearned to learn as a child but could not because Dad refused to allow us to learn a musical instrument. Music was in my blood and dancing was my means of expressing it. I would sometimes be reminded of my first dance another lifetime ago, of the freedom I allowed myself when my brother and I had to sneak to a dance, thinking of my whole life ahead of me.

"Mis tres cuadros," three pictures, symbolized the Spanish-speaking cultures throughout the world, my culture, and my life. The children and the *viejo* were the joy, happiness, and blessed ignorance of the young, as well as the tribulations of the suffering and toils of the old. They were realities that refused to be hidden by the flourish of someone's brush strokes.

The distant rhythms of a *cumbia* disappeared when a man's voice broke through my off-key humming. He identified himself as being with the State Department and continued on to utter the most significant statement I had heard since my dad had announced he was going to give me $100 so I could go to college. It completely prevented any clear thoughts for the rest of the day. The heck with finishing next week's lesson plans . . . the man told me I was seriously being considered for the position of ambassador to Honduras!

No matter how much I try thinking back to exactly what I said after that, all I remember was stammering and stuttering and then hearing myself utter the profound words, "Who? Me? No, I don't think I can."

His response was, "Why don't you think about it seriously over the weekend and I'll call you again on Monday? However, in the meantime, whatever you do, do not discuss this with anyone other than your doctor or your husband. Under any circumstances!"

I was shaking so hard. I could hardly put the receiver of the phone back on its cradle. I could have sworn the walls of my tiny, cramped office had just moved inward another foot. Suddenly breathing became difficult. Me? An ambassador? Someone had to be pulling my leg. April Fool's Day had been only a few days ago. I had received a call that day too and that caller had told me I had been selected as a distinguished citizen of New Mexico. I didn't believe that call either until two days later when I read about myself in the paper and realized it was true. It was only then that I sent the requested additional documentation to the committee that had been requested.

But this guy had given me telephone numbers to call if I had any questions. The icing on the cake was that I could call collect. Now that is impressive to a college professor. The more I thought about it, the more perplexed I became. Maybe he was for real.

I called my husband, whose office was in the adjacent building but sounded silly trying to tell him "in code" what had just happened. He was polite enough to say, "Look, Mari-Luci, it's eleven o'clock. Why don't we go home where we can talk?" He didn't add the "and please make sense" that I was expecting to hear.

I barely took time to turn off the swamp cooler that had been added to most of the professors' offices for comfort. I looked upon it fondly as my "duster." Every time I turned it on, the dust would move around along with any papers not firmly trapped down by piles of books. I left the ancient venetian blinds up so the profusion of green plants that personally identified my office could get their daily dose of sunlight, and with my purse in hand and a lot of doubts in my head, I left for the parking lot.

Meeting Heri at our Mercedes, (I always had a beautiful sleek, fast car these days), with our typical hug and kiss, I tried to tell him everything that had happened in one sentence. "Wait," he said raising his hands in his typical expressive way in defense of my newest bombardment of occurrences, "Start at the beginning." Within the ten minutes it took to get to our house, I was finally able to untangle my words enough to tell him everything that had transpired. He continued to ask questions during my rendition and I tried to answer them even though my mind was racing at a hundred miles an hour.

All of a sudden I blurted out, "Of course, even if the call is for real, I could never accept!"

Pulling into the driveway at that same moment, he turned to face me with an expression of total disbelief on his face and said the words I dared not hope to hear, "What? What do you mean?"

I couldn't believe my ears. I said as calmly as I could, considering the pace at which my heart was pounding and the pain in my breathing, "What would happen to you if I accepted?" A hundred things were racing through my mind. He was a Latino—a macho—it was unheard of for the man to stay home and the woman to go off to work. Our life was too traditional; we were traditional Hispanics. How could I ask him to give up the job he loved so I could get a crack at the big time? I didn't have the skills to be a political figure; I was just a shoemaker's daughter who had become a first-grade teacher and through sheer luck had been hired at the university.

I was pulled back down to earth when his strong, deep voice finally broke through the personal argument building momentum inside me. In his natural but polite native Colombian manners, Heri insisted in sincerity, "Mari-Luci, you must accept. Don't you understand? Your president is calling you. Don't worry about me. I'm a secure person. If I don't find a job, I'll write. I'll find something to do. You must accept when your call comes Monday. It's a great honor. You cannot let this opportunity pass by. Tell your president you will be honored to be considered."

So that was that. From that instant on, there was never any doubt in either of our minds that I would accept if the call was legitimate and I was selected.

The weekend crawled slowly along and by Monday, I was an anxiety attack waiting to happen. I hung out in my office all morning hoping for the phone to ring. My usually open door which meant my office would be full of students either borrowing books, sharing ideas on dissertation subjects, or even sometimes finding in me a sympathetic ear to lean on, was closed. The newspaper I used to cover my window was securely taped in place. I always loved and welcomed my students and their time in my office was what I loved most about a professor's life, but today I needed the quiet time. I was waiting for the call that would change my life.

While watching the minute hand moving around and around the clock, I scrutinized my office as if for the first time while contemplating how I had ended up there. The office had been converted from a former dorm room. It had two large closets which took up most of the precious space but were almost useless because they were built in rooms with high ceilings. The radiator under the window had become an old friend with its humming and clanging from its efforts to heat the office. The various uneven shelves were scavenged from other offices or discarded because they were too ugly for someone else to use. But even with their disfigurement, I regarded them fondly and had arranged them in an artistic way, familiar with my mother's style of making something out of nothing. My inherent need for organization found me always sorting the books perched on them, making sure they were categorized by subject matter. They were there for my students, specifically for them to use whenever they needed them. I guess the struggles I had felt in my early years as a student when I had to negotiate and barter for books were reflected in my generosity with my prized possessions, because I never denied a student any book that he or she required. The students even lent the books to each other. But despite the many hands that held them and as many places as they found themselves, amazingly enough, almost all of my books always found their way home to my shelves, though never in the right place.

Finally the phone rang with the awaited call. Trying to keep myself composed and not allow my utterance to sound as if I was a total bundle of nervousness, I told "the voice" that I would be honored if the president considered me for the position and I agreed to his request of undergoing a thorough check of all the activities of my entire lifetime.

Though the weekend had been long and difficult because of the waiting and the wondering about the validity of the call, it was nothing compared with what was to come. His request of complete secrecy while I was being investigated was excruciatingly difficult. First, we were Latinos and *la familia*, the family, is the most important aspect of our lives. I would have felt better if we could have just shared the news with at least my mother and sister. And there were our extremely close friends. They should know I was being considered. Besides, they would find out when the FBI started investigating me, wouldn't they? What excuse would I give them when they were asked questions? And then, of course, there were my students. I couldn't exclude them. Now they would have to find other professors to guide them in their dissertation writing.

I felt a familiar twinge with that one. I was deserting my students—what awful, guilty feelings! I had felt the same way fifteen years before when I had been asked to instruct at the university while I was teaching first grade. It was hard then to leave those precious students to someone else when I regarded them as mine only. And now I was leaving my current exceptional students without my guidance and help. I had a moral obligation to remain with them for the duration of my contract, didn't I? In retrospect, how vain could that thought be? Surely they would live through it and maybe find someone who could help them even more.

Had I left anyone out that should be told right away? As a youngster, I had been taught to share experiences, especially the good kind. And here was the most exciting thing that had ever happened to me and we were supposed to be silent.

Despite the difficulty and guilt that came with it in doing so, we kept the secret. In the weeks to come, I received dozens of calls from Washington. And each time "they," the faceless voices, would remind me not to discuss the nomination because it could disqualify me from further consideration. Some of these "voices" became my friends and I hoped someday I would have a face to match the voice. They were always helpful and answered the dozens of questions I would generate between calls, but never did anyone give me an iota of assurance that I would be selected. I always wondered if my silence and the display of outward calm I had to maintain were the first tests I must pass to prove that I could keep national and international secrets and face any challenges that came with an ambassadorship. If I could keep calm and quiet about my nomination, I could keep quiet about anything!

That summer of 1977 was the first time in my fifteen-year university career that I didn't teach. Instead, I coped by cleaning, sorting, and using reams of paper in preparation for fall classes, just in case. I had my doubts about this whole thing anyway. After all, I was not rich nor a politician. I was a humble person with a humble lifestyle and didn't even own an evening dress! Surely wealth and fame were prerequisites for the job.

Despite my doubts, my husband wasn't idle at all. He was absolutely sure I would be selected. So at home, we started cleaning the yard, the garden shed, the garage, and all the closets in the house. It's amazing how much one can accumulate that one doesn't need. Even if I didn't get appointed, at least our house and offices would be clean.

All this activity was hush-hush. The tension was building up to almost unbearable degrees. I could hardly concentrate on the preparation of my classes and began a new worry about leaving my mother and grandmother still living two-hundred-miles away in Las Vegas. Elvira and my brother-in-law, who lived in Albuquerque, would have to take care of Mom and Nanita without our help. It didn't end there, though. Could I handle being separated from them? I needed to be near them physically. My familia was my sustenance. Their importance and significance had been bred into me from my earliest childhood. Being with them was as much a part of me as breathing. I was so confused. My loyalty to my family was complete and unquestionable and I was always with them. But at the same time, I wanted this appointment very much. My insides were filled with the conflict of it and for the second time in my life, I felt I was betraying part of who I was, just as I did when I had decided to divorce my first husband and felt I wasn't being a loyal Catholic.

Those four months of waiting became agony. Besides keeping the secret, we were constantly reminded not to initiate any move. "Don't rent your house. Don't start shopping. Don't have garage sales," the voices would harp endlessly. "Even if your nomination is accepted, the Senate might not confirm it," they would say.

We almost became recluses. Instead of socializing with our friends, we stayed home and studied everything we could on Honduras, checking out library books feverishly. My medical papers had to be sent to Washington twice. (At least my doctor knew!) They had lost them and when they called the third time requesting my medical records, I knew something was wrong. One of my new friends did some tracking, locating the first set that had been sent, but this still caused a delay, holding up my appointment several weeks. The Congress had gone into a congressional recess and I had to wait until their return before they could act on my nomination.

Weeks later, after my husband and I had finally been cleared through scrutiny of loyalty, political contributions, income tax, friends, acquaintances, legal standing, health status, and police records, we were jubilant to find out what a good American I was. Heri was still a Colombian citizen, but he must have been in good standing too.

Even though we were cleared, the wait continued. The calls became fewer and fewer. Maybe the decision had been made not to nominate me and they just forgot to tell me. I began to believe that I wasn't going to be nominated. Oh well, my syllabi and class assignments were ready and waiting.

With the traditional fall greetings letter, schedules, and requests for meetings and such to be attended from our college dean, school reconvened. I was actually looking forward to this first day and the busy days to follow with committee meetings and student advising. I was tired of waiting and wondering and worrying. On my first day back while walking past the administrative secretary's office, two graduate assistants ran out, warning me that three TV stations had called and that I was to return their calls immediately. The secretary joined them and I pleaded with her to keep reporters away from me. She knew my intense dislike for publicity. She had kept them away from me before when I was involved in campus doings that were "newsworthy." She promised to do her best.

I practically ran into my office. Could I have been nominated? How had the media found out? We had told no one and no one had told us. The leak had to have come from Washington. What should I do now? What should I say? The chairperson of the department walked in and said, "What's this I hear about you becoming an ambassador?"

The months of conditioning to keep silent persisted and without missing a beat and adding a shrug of my shoulder for good measure, I said, "Next, they'll say I'm being considered to run for the Senate . . . you know rumors." After a little small talk, he left convinced, I hoped.

The telephone call I made to my husband was like déjà vu. "It's leaked," I gasped. "Let's go home." While grabbing my purse, the phone started ringing, but I was afraid to answer it. So I ran down to the parking lot instead, not looking anyone in the face for fear they would ask me something, which is totally out of character for a Southwesterner. Once again my husband met me at our car and we cut the ten-minute drive home down by several minutes.

The phone there too was ringing off the hook. I wouldn't let Heri answer it. I just knew it was a reporter and I didn't want to lie. No one in Washington had coached me on this scenario. We sat there thinking of smart answers that wouldn't give anything away. The phone continued to ring. I finally announced that I would call Washington as soon as the phone stopped ringing. They would tell me what to do. Heri kept insisting that the phone ringing probably was Washington anyway but I pleaded with him not to pick it up. Impulsively he stood up and answered it. He grew a smile that spread a mile and handed the phone to me. "It's for you. It's Washington."

The "voice" congratulated me on my nomination and asked if there had been any inconvenience caused because the president had announced it before I had been notified. I thought to myself, "Only slightly; I almost had a heart attack." But to the voice I said, "Oh, not at all." It seemed they hadn't been able to contact me before the announcement had been placed on the president's desk and it was too late to retract it. The nation had heard about it before I had.

After hanging up, we tried to regain our composure. We were ecstatic. We returned to campus immediately, foregoing any lunch. Who could eat at a time like this? We went to the dean's office and told him first and then other close friends, answering questions as best we could. I still wasn't sure how much information to volunteer because the Senate still had to approve the nomination. So I didn't comment much on the last four months of silent agony and we restricted our answers to the many questions to general comments only. The rest of the day was declared "una gran fiesta." It was a blur of *abrazos*, *besos*, salutations, and even calls from complete strangers. The flowers began arriving sometime after two o'clock in the afternoon and were overflowing out of my office and at home. The phone never stopped ringing but now I could answer it. We had no idea we had so many friends. It was a beautiful feeling.

The TV stations were held back by the university press until the following morning when I would give my first press conference. Even though I had now spent years doing public speaking, a television interview was a brand new experience for me and I kept referring to it as a "meeting." Though not very sophisticated, it sounded less formal and scary. I was still shy and every inch of my body was trembling. I knew I would learn soon enough to fulfill my role as ambassador and I made that promise sincerely to all New Mexicans watching the news broadcast.

My jubilation was short lived. I entered into another new phase of worrying. Now it was, What will happen if the Senate doesn't approve my nomination? The whole world will know I failed the test. I still had to be the best student with a halo perched on top of my head. I had no idea what questions they would ask me at my hearing. Nightmares pursued my dreams in the weeks that followed. I would wake up exhausted, feeling as if I had lived it instead of just dreamed it. The recent Watergate hearings were ever present in the back of my mind. So many people had been drilled in those hearings in front of the entire nation on supposed bribes and illegal telephone taps during the last presidential elections. I would visualize the Senate committee members seated high up around a semicircular table, looming huge and ominous, with me sitting down below. They would be drilling me with questions I couldn't answer as relentlessly as in the Watergate hearings. There I would be, trembling, all alone, and not even remembering my name. So I continued studying everything I could get my hands on with a fever, along with a hundred other things I could now do openly to prepare myself unexhaustedly for the biggest, most important test of my life.

With the secret finally out, I was able at last to go visit my family in Las Vegas to tell them all the details of my nomination. Neighbors greeted us as we pulled up outside Mom's small adobe home nestled in the center of her glorious garden filled with shades of fall colors. Still uncertain how to respond to all the attention as neighbors continued to congratulate me, I would just reply, "Thanks, but maybe the Senate won't confirm me."

One of the hardest conversations I would ever have in my life was explaining to my mother that I might be leaving the States for a long time. Ever since I had left Las Vegas, I had made sure we visited her at least twice a month regardless of the effort it took. But now I was sitting in her front room, which was much more modern than when we were children, telling her I had no idea if I would see her for one or two years. I kept toying with her hand-crocheted doilies covering all the tables in my state of nervousness. Family is something Chicanos don't take lightly.

Telling my kids about my new adventure was a breeze. Being university students and deeply immersed in their studies, they took it in stride. Knowing their mother all too well with the energy I always demonstrated, they didn't say much more than, "Gee, Mom, that's great. Congratulations." They were happy for me, of course, but couldn't quite understand how I had gotten the job. While they all said they might visit, only one and his wife would actually make it.

The hardest person to tell was Nanita, who was now ninety-six years old. I knew deep down I would never see her again. Her long years of struggle had finally taken their toll and she was becoming weak and infirm as the elderly eventually do. Heri asked Nanita what she thought an ambassador was. She hesitated some, apologizing and offering excuses for her forgetfulness, and answered in her high-pitched, squeaky voice, "El embajador representa al Presidente de Los Estados Unidos en otro país," which in English means, "an ambassador represents the President of the United States in another country." I was proud of Nanita for her intelligence despite her lack of formal education. She had only made it through second grade and her explanation was more accurate than some of the ones we had heard from people who claimed to be well educated.

After praising her intelligence for her first answer with abrazos and besos, Heri once again tested her by asking her where Honduras was. After an explanation of her geography and history lessons in school some ninety years ago, she recalled Honduras being somewhere rather close to Mexico. Again, we were astounded because the most frequently asked question we had received about Honduras was, "Where is British Honduras?" We continually had to explain to people that we weren't referring to British Honduras, but Honduras in Central America. I would wonder a long time after leaving that day if my grandmother was exceptionally brilliant, or if the schools ninety years ago were exceptionally good.

With the excitement demonstrated by our family and friends for my new position, and my sister's continued reassurance that she would take care of Mom and Nanita, I finally began to feel a little more at ease about leaving New Mexico and it was easier to focus on the many preparations for the anticipated move to Honduras. I was invited by the Department of State to go to Washington, D.C., to attend some meetings related to the

Panama Canal treaty negotiations. Because most of the heads of government of Latin America were scheduled to be there, I found this a unique opportunity to begin immersing myself in the political reality of Latin America and readily accepted the invitation.

I had made previous trips to Washington, both as a tourist and attendee at many educational conferences, staying in nice hotels, but none compared with the Washington Hilton where I was accommodated. I had walked by it previously, admiring the beautiful façade and front gardens, but never dreamed I would ever stay there, much less mingle with diplomats from countries around the world. It was explained to me that the government didn't usually allow per diem for such luxurious accommodations, but that this was a special occasion and allowances had been made so that the diplomats from the United States could be closer to the foreign dignitaries.

The week I was there was filled with constant activity. I was allowed to get acquainted with non-classified material on Honduras, but because my appointment as ambassador was not yet confirmed by the Senate, I was not considered "official" and couldn't attend signing ceremonies or any other official functions. I was allowed, however, to meet the chief of state of Honduras. I was driven to Andrews Air Force Base in a limousine and actually stood in the receiving line with all the dignitaries to greet General Melgar Castro.

As he went down the line of about thirty dignitaries, shaking hands with each one, I was introduced perfunctorily by a protocol officer. He shook my hand warmly and moved onto the next person. He suddenly did a double take, moving back to me and saying, "Oh, Ambassador Jaramillo," and proceeded to give me a warm Latino abrazo. Believe me, Latino hugs are the best. They show great emotion and tell you the giver is happy to be in your presence. Never does one feel that Latino hugs are given out of obligation or habit. I was delighted and knew from that moment on that we were going to be good friends. He took time out, making the others down the line wait for their acknowledgment to tell me that Honduran officials had studied my credentials and heartily approved of me. He then added a little more icing to the cake by saying they were anticipating my arrival. True to his word and my hunch, in the next few years, we spent much time together.

Boy, could anything be better than that? My heart pounded and I was so excited that I could feel my characteristic tears beginning to water up my eyes. Surely, I thought to myself right then and there, if the Honduran president wants me, the Senate Foreign Relations Committee will approve of me. But I held myself in check while all the cautions that Department of State officials had given me about taking Senate confirmation for granted rose to the surface of my consciousness.

After the chief of state's impromptu remarks at the base, we were all led to waiting cars. The charge rode with him and I rode in an unmarked car. But just having seen him and talked with him was a thrill for me. Thank you, Baby Jesus.

Even though this week in Washington was very historic, I concentrated little on the Panama Canal. Instead, I initiated my own briefings. Since I live to learn, it was not difficult for me to find out quickly which files I could read and which people I could talk to and set about accomplishing this task immediately. The Department of State set up a series of courtesy calls, which I went to even though I would rather have been studying in preparation for my confirmation hearing. They were time consuming but necessary. As a newcomer to a bureaucracy, I knew these personal contacts would help me when I was in the field and that they would assist me later whenever I needed help.

The evening I had been looking forward to the most finally arrived. It was a beautiful dinner in the Jefferson room at the Department of State. This was the most exciting but also the most important event for me because I would be meeting many ambassadors and other important people from both Washington and Latin America. I was fortunate to have the minister of foreign relations from the Honduran government as my dinner partner and I used the occasion to learn much about the people and current events in Honduras.

I was prepared for a formal dinner, but this had been the most formal one I had ever attended. I had acquired an evening dress of navy chiffon with a capelet for the occasion, feeling that I had mastered the necessary protocol. However, when the salad was brought after the main course, I was surprised but managed not to let it show and made no comment. But I knew the waiter would get in trouble and my heart went out to him before I noticed all the waiters had made the same mistake! For once, it was good that I kept my mouth shut. Dinner was held "as the French do it." Salad comes last. They would faint with consternation if they were in the Southwest for dinner. We common folk always had salad first or with our meal. So much for that; I made a mental note to include Emily Post in my instructional curriculum on dos and don'ts.

The week went by quickly and all too soon I was back in Albuquerque. Several of the voices I had come to know as friends in Washington finally had been given a face to match. But time had been much too short and even though we knew so much about each other through phone conversations, we had barely begun to get acquainted in person. This irritation was put from my mind as I prepared to participate in a brand new activity.

An impressive banquet had been arranged for the "New Mexican presidential appointees" and I had been invited as one of the honored guests. Attendance at a party with a political flavor was new for me, or rather, I hadn't been to one since I had accompanied my grandfather to precinct meetings in Las Vegas when I was six or seven years old. Wearing another newly acquired evening dress, which meant I now actually owned two gowns, I was ready just in case I had to make a speech. Typical of me, I had in my purse a copy of the brief remarks I had given at the swearing-in ceremony. I ended up making my short comments, but I was in such awe of all the important people there that I didn't remember what I had said once I sat down. I still could not consider myself important. I was simply Mari-Luci, the Mexican immigrant's daughter.

I was again called to Washington only a week later. My briefings this time had a much more formal tone. My appointments were scheduled for every half-hour or for every hour of the day, which in Washington includes noontime appointments. Used to this type of scheduling, I fell right into the pattern. Thank goodness recall has been one of my fortes. Remembering the new faces and names of people I was meeting wasn't a problem and several individuals were impressed when I would greet them by name in a café or office.

The briefings were excellent and I gathered information that would be extremely helpful to me. Since Honduras is a country considered "disaster prone," especially because of hurricanes, the briefing on how the United States helps in disasters would prove in the future to be very useful. But there seemed to be a mystique surrounding my briefings. I couldn't understand it. So much of the information now being shared with me would be useful for all Americans to know because they would understand our foreign policies so much better. But at nearly every briefing, I was told that the information was classified in one way or another and since I hadn't been approved yet by the hearing committee, I had yet to attend a "secret" one. Those would wait until my Senate confirmation . . . always a shadow that followed me as a reminder that I could still end up returning to campus instead of moving to Honduras.

Ten days had passed before I completed the rigid schedule they had put me on. Most of the people I met had had long careers in the foreign service and were very knowledgeable about world affairs. After being consistently introduced to these people as a "political appointee," I couldn't imagine how this term applied to me. I had thought of myself as a "presidential appointee." After joking with several people about it, I realized that the term was used to separate those from the "in-group," that is the Foreign Service, from the outsiders. I, of course was

from the latter group. But there were no hostilities and I was
treated the same as newly appointed Foreign Service ambassadors who were going through the same briefings.

It was an easy time for me and I adapted and learned quickly. The only difficult thing for me was the famous and important
people I would continually see. I was as awestruck as a teenager
when the Soviet Foreign Minister and Russian ambassador to the
United States, Andrei Andreyevich Gromyko, walked by, and
later that week I also saw Moshe Dayan from Israel; it was all I
could do to contain myself and not run after them for an auto-
graph. The Department of State was a magic land and I was a
princess who had landed in the middle of it, stepping down from
my pumpkin carriage. I wished all Americans could experience
what I had. It would do the morale of the country good.

The formal hearing that would confirm me as an ambassador
continued to be postponed. The committee was involved in
important canal work the entire week. When I was finally told that
the day had come for me to go for my confirmation hearing, I
don't remember ever having been as nervous in my entire life. Heri
had stayed in Albuquerque because we had been told his expenses
would not be covered until the swearing-in ceremony and we
weren't sure we could afford his airfare because there were going
to be other expenses we might have to cover. I was scared to death
and totally alone. What would happen to me under other kinds of
pressures I imagined ambassadors would go through? Would I be
as nervous as I was now at being asked a few simple questions?
What business did I have being here if I couldn't even handle this?

The new suede suit I had specially picked out for this occasion after careful observation of "professional" Foreign Service
women in the State Department was much too warm. I hadn't yet
read the book on how professional women should dress and wondered if it would give me instructions on how not to perspire in
hot, humid climates. What I wouldn't have given at that moment
for my simple skirts and cotton blouses that were the normal
dress for women back home in New Mexico!

When the questioning began, I thought I was going to make it to home plate smoothly and professionally when a member of the committee just had to ask, "And what makes you think you are going to be a good ambassador when you have only been a school teacher?" Now anyone who knows a teacher knows that teachers are very proud of their profession and that one should never make the mistake of saying we are "just" teachers. All my nervousness, fears, doubts, and anxieties left me as if I had stepped up to the chalkboard in my first grade class. I'm surprised I didn't stand up on the table and use it as an improvised bandwagon when I began whipping off the qualifications I hadn't even thought about before that very instant. Finally stopping for breath, I saw the smiles on their faces and knew I could stop my defense.

Once safely installed back in my hotel room, I called my family to share the great news and just as on the day when I received the first phone call that started all of this, I don't think I made much sense. But I was able to convey to my family that I had been appointed and they were, in turn, ecstatically happy.

In one sense, the days moved with lightning speed after that, but in another, they dragged almost as painfully as the previous four months. The swearing-in ceremony had been postponed twice because the assistant secretary of state was not available at the times when it had been originally scheduled. When the date was finally confirmed, I called Heri to tell him, "Hurry up and get here. It's finally happening." Again, I was expected to stand up and give a speech, but as I began to put my pencil to my ever-familiar yellow lined notepad, I was handed an impromptu speech by my desk officer of things I might wish to say. No one had ever assisted with any of my speeches and this was a welcome surprise.

By hinting instead of direct comments, the officers in charge of the swearing-in ceremonies let me know that I would be expected to hold a reception at the swearing-in-ceremony. It was the tradition and was expected. So, along with everything else I was catching on to, I investigated what exactly "expected" meant. I was learning quickly the ropes of hidden meanings, elusive statements, and how to avoid making a direct point and wanted to make sure I got this one right! The expected reception turned out to be finger foods and fine wines.

After discovering that the Jefferson Room in the Department of State was used, I then found out that only certain caterers were allowed and when quoted prices for such a reception, my guest list decreased significantly while the bill increased tremendously. With a guest list of only thirty people, it would cost me more than we had ever spent for entertaining in our home. Our finances had already been drained because while I was flying back and forth, staying in hotels, catching taxi trips, purchasing appropriate clothing, and now hosting a reception, I had been reimbursed for none of it and my idea that ambassadorships were for the wealthy seemed to be proving itself. I decided right then and there that when my tour of duty was over, I would remind people, perhaps from my bandwagon, that middle-class Americans can be ambassadors because of their knowledge, but if they don't have a substantial checking account, the initial expenses could put them in tremendous debt.

Practicing my diplomacy, I started asking when my pay would begin since no one had mentioned it. My pretext was that my university had to be notified in order to initiate the paperwork that would have to be done before I left the country. However, it turned out that we would already be in Honduras before anyone ever seriously talked to me about salary, insurance, and other requirements of the new job.

My swearing-in finally arrived and I gave the "required" remarks that had been prepared for me. With the addition of the usual comments, which I had perfected to "grab hold" of even the most hostile crowd, the audience of State Department officials, reporters, and my few friends couldn't resist smiling. It was important to me that even though I was now considered one of them, they knew this ambassador would retain her sense of humor and never forget where she came from!

Still not used to my short business dress, my continued tugging at my skirt and the bad hangnail, which was hidden with an unsightly Band-Aid, were the only hitches in the ceremony. After all the pledges were made, the female protocol officer led me to a historic desk to sign a document. As she handed me the pen, she whispered in my ear, "Your hand is shaking." Without realizing that my next words would be the icebreaker for the festivities to commence, I answered quite loudly from my nervousness, "That isn't the only thing shaking!" The party was on.

The last few days in Washington included more briefings and also inoculations that we had not already received in Albuquerque, which included very long needles! Mosquitoes and fleas are a given in Latin America, just as they are in any area that is hot and humid, and they love to eat only me, so I inquired about a shot to help. Since it would take a long series of desensitization shots, I knew I would have to grow immune "on the job" and gave up on that one. I was in a hurry to begin my new life! This red tape was just taking too long.

People began calling me Madame Ambassador and my husband Dr. Jaramillo. One of my new highly respected friends cautioned me to always insist on the titles. This was probably one of the hardest things for me to accept because of my informal, friendly nature. I would pretend that it was natural when someone would address me that way, but every inch of me wanted to say, "Please, just call me Mari-Luci." They also stood up when I entered a room. It was very awkward for me. I had spent the last several years preaching about equality and now people were standing at attention when I arrived. But the words of my friend never left my mind and I went with the flow.

The minute we were allowed to leave Washington to return home for the last time, we made the reservations and flew out. We were now "famous" and I continually tried to downplay it while my husband was constantly reminding me that I now represented President Carter and that was a great honor. But it was still difficult for me to understand and think that I should behave differently because I was now "famous."

Parties and visits from friends overtook my home. One of them would become a traditional Mexican fiesta, complete with—you guessed it—more speeches! Incidents throughout the duration of my life were recalled by all the people I knew, both personally and professionally. I had no idea that I was so nice and those telltale tears rolled down my face. This quickly brought on another reflection in which one of my closest friends stood up and said, "We don't have to worry that Mari-Luci will ever change. She will always show her feelings." I was really embarrassed by that one, for while I was touched by the thought, I felt sure that ambassadors weren't supposed to cry. Oh, how I hated my "tearing."

In quiet moments and even busy ones, I had many moments of self-doubt. Would I like the new job? Would the Hondurans like me? Would my skills be sufficient to handle what was to come? My self-inflicted torture was thinking about all that could go wrong instead of concentrating on the skills I had told the Senate Foreign Relations Committee I possessed. My self confidence flew out the window, but at least my humor remained.

It would have been so much easier if we had been able to initiate the packing, storing, and shipping of our household items months ago, but back then it was still a secret. Our car was on the list for shipping. Even though I would always have to be chauffeured wherever I went in a limousine while there, Heri would be able to use our car.

Though we knew easy ways of getting to and from Latin America, the travel woman with the Department of State in Washington had informed me that we would travel only on American airlines, and that it should be tourist, not first class. Her suggestion, which was really a "you are not free to do as you please anymore" reminder, turned our one-day trip into three because we had to travel first from Albuquerque to Houston overnight, into Guatemala for another night, and finally to Tegucigalpa on the third day.

After many months of agonized waiting, unable to do or say anything, and then the last few hectic weeks of beelike activity, we boarded the plane. Our four suitcases which were so old that two of them had to be tied with nylon rope, were so heavy that Heri was forced to pay a hefty sum for the extra weight.

As the plane took off, Heri and I shared a hand squeeze and *beso* for luck and I dug into my briefcase for my list of "to-dos." Amazingly enough, the only thing we had forgotten was extra socks for Heri and hairspray for me. We decided that our overnight stay in Houston would provide us with an opportunity to purchase those things and we settled into our seats for a few hours of nothing more hectic than the humming of engines.

Houston found us staying in a hotel for the "not so rich and famous" instead of one considered suitable for an ambassador. This ambassador wasn't rich and didn't want to be famous and she stayed at a normal hotel! The bad part about it was that it was located far away from town. There was no opportunity to pick up the things we had forgotten. So I decided that hairspray only hurt the environment and that I could do without it, and since I had been darning socks from the age of eight, this ambassador could still darn those of her husband. After all, in all my Washington briefings, that was one thing I hadn't been told I could or couldn't do, so I assumed it was still OK.

The next day we were in Guatemala City where we didn't know to check in with the U.S. Embassy. The Department of State hadn't briefed me on travel protocol and we had been forced to make our own arrangements, so there was much that had been overlooked. So we drove around the picturesque city in a taxi instead of a limousine and had no bodyguard to protect me in my new position. I felt perfectly safe, though, because I still considered myself an ordinary citizen, having a hard time remembering my status.

The third day we finally arrived for our new life, late but safe. These last few days had been spent with so much anticipation that the excitement had caused sleep to elude me almost completely. But as we flew over the beautiful country, I didn't feel tired at all. Instead, a feeling of euphoria had replaced the fatigue. The plane landed and we stepped out into the sunshine and all the anguish and worry of the last four months faded away within seconds to nothing more than a dim memory. I said a prayer to el Santo Niño, tugged on my seven-year-old long-sleeved, hot, navy-blue dress, and went to work.

chapter

Madame Ambassador

Even though there was no emergency, the sirens were wailing as the police escort guided the motorcade traveling at the pace of a whirlwind toward el Palacio del Gobierno. Their high-pitched sound created a sense of urgency, and the flags snapping in the wind of the speeding black sedans as they wove their way up and down the hilly and winding streets seemed totally in concert with my excitement and apprehension.

The commotion created as we drove through the streets drew people out of their homes and stopped others on their way to destinations only known to them. As these people stood or made a seat out of the sidewalk to watch the show, I caught my first glimpse of some of the poverty I would be up against when I began my official duties in only a matter of an hour or so. Not all of the observers were poor people. Some of them were obviously middle-class citizens. If they had been standing on a corner in a suburb of the United States, you would not be able to discern any difference between them and us. But many of the people watching us pass were dressed in clothing that was worn and dirty, and their faces were smudged and tired. As I looked at some of the children with their big, round eyes,

I thought of my own childhood and my flour sack dresses and considered myself fortunate. After all, I had always had a roof over my head, a bed to sleep on, and clean, cold, and delicious water. These children may not have experienced some of those things that even I had taken for granted. Poverty is relative and maybe that is why so many of us take the condition for granted. It's easy to overlook.

My deputy chief of mission (DCM), was riding with me in my limousine while Heri followed in the one just behind us. So any reassurance from my husband about the upcoming event was not forthcoming. I was totally on my own. I knew there was to be no podium I could use to support my wobbly knees and I carried no speech, so I didn't even have any papers to use as a security blanket. But even these setbacks were not enough to deter me from the excitement I was feeling. I actually had goose bumps! I tried concentrating on the view outside the two-inch-thick bulletproof tinted windows, but didn't have much luck. So I began to reflect on how I had conquered my fear when I recited my Halloween poem in front of my teacher's friends centuries ago and decided that if there were any refreshments on the table, I could focus on them rather than looking directly at people if I had to speak. It had worked for me when I was eight. It could work now.

The sirens and the DCM's voice reassuring me that the ceremony was going to be brief were blended together into a kind of background noise that wasn't quite real. Neither was the guard directly sitting in front of me. He and one other young man had already become constant shadows, following or leading me, but always the closest to me no matter where I was. They were both very nice and quite handsome, and while they would never don a uniform in the three years they were with me, I knew a handgun would always be carefully concealed within their immaculate outfits. The only tangible evidence that I had to cling to that this trek toward the center of government was not a dream, was that same old navy blue dress that had become my basic uniform in

the last few ceremonies. Its familiarity and the way it continually climbed up my hips kept reminding me that this was for real.
Every time I would think, There it goes, and, what have I gotten
myself into?

The answer to my repeated question to myself was that after
having only three days in Honduras to get acquainted with my
new position, staff, and luxurious surroundings, I was speeding
on my way to present my credentials to the president of the
Republic of Honduras. At last, my position was about to become
official. I would now begin my real work and anything I did from
this day forward would be my legacy as to what kind of ambassador I was going to be.

As I had left the residence for the government palace, I
sensed the same undercurrent of excitement I was feeling in the
residence staff. They had all gathered together in the front entry
to wish me luck and see me off. In our short time together, we
had already been establishing a rapport of friendliness and gen-
uineness. They had learned quickly that I did not view myself as
above anyone and that I would not treat them with any disrespect
or overbearance. They could now establish a consistent routine,
which had been missing along with an ambassador. Because of
changes in U.S. political parties and the attention on the Panama
Canal treaty discussions, there had been no time for the drawn-
out process of selecting one before now. But while I was easygo-
ing, I knew they were able to recognize that my mission was one
I took very seriously. They did not yet know I would only be satisfied with results and not with the standard line used by pro-
crastinators: "I'm working on it."

I had long ago determined what my goals would be. I so badly
wanted to be a good ambassador. No, that's not true. I wanted to
be an excellent one. Perhaps one of the best American ambassadors Honduras had ever experienced. Could it be possible? I'd
give it my best. My personal goal was to get everyone, regardless
of social class, thinking and talking about human rights. This was
the platform my president, Jimmy Carter, was expounding, and to

which I had devoted my life, although I had never called my work "human rights." But I knew these human rights had guided my life and now I had a wonderful name for them. I thought if I helped get a great dialogue going, the Hondurans themselves would institute laws and activities that would perhaps lead toward the beginning of a working democracy.

The State Department had given me several goals to work on, but mainly they wanted me to work on two broad ones. They encouraged me to "move" Honduras toward democracy and look for ways to help settle the border issue with El Salvador. [Author's aside: "The main issues were resolved, and I represented our country when the peace treaty was signed by the two countries, several months after I had left Honduras."] Both were huge assignments and I would try to find ways to meet these goals during every waking moment. I knew I would be able to accomplish many things, but if I couldn't move these two quickly along, I would consider myself a failure regardless of what the State Department said.

There were so many important things to be done. However, I had received in the last few days in Honduras and during my stay in Washington, frequent hints that I was expected to redecorate the residence. In general, the upkeep of the house was part of a regular assignment, but as much as I love to decorate, I couldn't see it as a priority. Oh-oh, maybe I should have brought a wife.

I had the prerogative to completely redecorate the residence and embassy offices. However, not only did I think it was inconsequential, but I also couldn't imagine spending money on such frivolous things. The directives from Washington and my personal goals were much more important than changing the color scheme of a room. Besides, the mansion was the most elegant house I had ever seen in my life, much less lived in. There was no need for any major changes. Its acres and acres of gardens full of banana plants and its orange, lemon, grapefruit, and avocado trees were full of beautiful birds. There were beds of cutting flowers everywhere you looked. The orchids that grew profusely in shady areas were beyond imagination and roses climbed wildly up the pink and pale green stone buildings and fences. There were sixteen gardeners alone just to take care of the outside gardens. Bougainvillea of every color of the rainbow lined a seemingly mile-long side of the road that wound gracefully up the hill to the mansion. The view was incredibly beautiful overlooking the entire city of Tegucigalpa, which means "silver hills."

The interior of the mansion was even more exquisite, beginning with the completely glassed in entryway. It was the perfect place for me to hang my social conscience and the etching of the Chicano farmer, which had traveled with me from my office at UNM, soon adorned the one solid wall. The wall was of the same pink-and-green native stone as the rest of the exterior of the mansion and the color highlighted the stark black-and-white lines of his face. Under my favorite picture was a small console, which, for the next three years, held a vase filled to capacity with beautiful flowers. The *viejito* was destined to become one of the best avenues I would have to strike up a conversation on my most important cause, the poor. Every single person that ever walked into that entryway would at some point comment on how interesting my farmer was and unknowingly open the door for me to breach this most sensitive subject.

The striking entryway led to a blanketed stairway of deep, rich red carpet fit for a queen to walk on and led on up to the entertaining part of the house. I would spend many a happy respite in the future during minutes of free time arranging and rearranging the beautiful white silk sofas, chairs, and footstools in those ornate cavernous rooms. Everything would always be strategically placed around the concert-sized grand piano which, because of its grandeur, was constantly moved around for effect. In the beginning before they got used to me, the staff would gasp at my rearranging efforts because "I shouldn't be doing physical labor." They would tell me, "No ambassador's wife has ever rearranged the way we have the furniture set. She just tells us where she wants it."

The subject ended quickly when I gently reminded them that "I'm not an ambassador's wife; I'm the ambassador and I personally enjoy rearranging furniture." They sighed, but accepted my answer, realizing how lucky they really were to have a *jefa*, a female boss, who, after all, really wasn't very finicky. I had come from a background of labor and they knew we were cut from the same cloth, which made it much easier to accept me. We soon became great "laborers" and worked as a team.

I had been instructed by the protocol officers, one from the United States and one from Honduras, on what to expect and do during this first upcoming ceremony I would participate in related to presenting my credentials. They explained to me that as soon as the president formally accepted me, I would immediately be thought of by the Hondurans as "Señora Embajadora" or in English, "Madame Ambassador." I was anxious to finally become official and felt ready to move forward, but as we neared the palace, the sight of the palace sentinels standing at attention outside the entrance upset me further. They did not move an inch and it seemed as if they didn't even blink. Since it was hot, any perspiration that gathered on their faces was left without wiping it off as if it wasn't even there. Their swords were unsheathed and crossed above their heads and the rays of the sun glinting off the shiny blades almost blinded us.

Presenting credentials is an extremely important task once an ambassador gets to the country he or she is assigned to. Sometimes, due to unforeseen circumstances, ambassadors have to wait before presenting theirs, but in my case, the country had been without an American ambassador for quite some time and the Honduran president had cleared his schedule at once to acknowledge me. The pageantry was incredible and it had been done solely in my honor! Imagine me representing the United States in a foreign country . . . a southwest Chicana who was also a shoemaker's daughter walking under the crossed swords of a hundred palace guards. I still couldn't quite believe it was happening.

I scooted out of the limousine as gracefully as my old graduation dress allowed, since it was creeping up again, and walked hurriedly with Heri, protocol officers, reporters, selected staff, my guard, presidential guards, and many others following behind me. We passed through corridors, large rooms, and finally to a beautifully ornate ballroom, all still lined with the untiring palace sentinels holding their swords crossed high above their heads.

The richness of the ballroom was stunning. In dim awareness, I absorbed the hand-carved gold scrollwork above the doors and around the twenty-foot tall windows. Paintings by famous artists hung on the pale blue walls and the hardwood floor was polished to such a sheen that it matched the swords of the palace guards. As I entered, the president was waiting for me beside the only three pieces of furniture at the far end of the room. I walked toward the nondescript table and two chairs. The closer I got, the larger that simple table became and before I reached the president, the table had turned into that same ominous desk the hearing committee had sat behind when I was first interviewed in Washington, D.C., for the job. I could have sworn it had grown teeth and was growling at me.

After I finally arrived at the other end of the ballroom where the president stood, which seemed to take a lifetime, we stood at attention while both national anthems were played. They both struck a chord of pride in my heart as I stood thinking about how I loved my country. I would always tear up when the "Star-Spangled Banner" was played, even at a football game. I knew I'd learn to love Honduras as I did my own country, but I did think their anthem was way too long!

At the end of the anthems, the president reached over, took my hand, and invited me to sit next to him. Lights were flashing all around us while the press took pictures of our handshake and I snuck in a good tug at my skirt as I sat down next to him for still more pictures. I was pleased that we had met once already in Washington while I was still undergoing my briefings.

General Melgar Castro was a cordial and warm man. Although he was a military officer, he was a populist and immediately instilled in people a liking for him. He was very jovial, with one of those million-dollar smiles à la President Carter that don't quit. In fact, during my tour of duty, there would be a cartoon published in the paper of General Castro, President Carter, and me with the same smile taking up half of our faces. I liked him immediately. He was shorter than I was and appeared slightly portly, but he held himself with military bearing and was still very handsome. He was confident, self-assured, and rich in personality—a great combination—and we would become very good friends for the remainder of his assignment. I became a regular visitor at the palace on business and enjoyed all the visits, even though some of them would be of a very serious nature.

His wife too would become a close acquaintance. She was immaculately groomed at all times. Her hair was beautifully coiffed and her nails were always manicured in bright colors. She paid great attention to every small detail. Latina women take their appearance very seriously and always dress to show their femininity. While the president's wife did this, she was also able to dress in a way that demonstrated that she was a woman with a purpose. Most first ladies find a cause during their husband's term in office, but this one was a pioneer. She was interested in the business world. She internalized an economic dream of prosperity for her country and though low key, talked about it often.

There would be a time when I would accompany her to Louisiana as her special guest while she spoke at a convention titled "Trade and the Woman in Business." She spoke about investing in Honduras and succeeded in making many aware of the great business opportunities there. She was very actively involved with the president and following his death several years after he left office, became the mayor of Tegucigalpa and later even a candidate for president. I didn't realize at the time how much of a politician she was herself.

A year or so after I arrived, the country experienced a coup that ousted General Castro as president, and both of them just disappeared from public life. People said that they had a big ranch and lived a life of luxury, so I wasn't concerned about their well-being. Many generals took turns that way. There was no meanness or killing or finding you in a grave. You just disappeared from public view. The army told them they weren't wanted anymore as the leaders of the country and sent them out to pasture.

Honduras had been ruled by the military for many years. Regardless of how one looked at it, it was ruled by a dictatorship. Everyone told me that the Honduran military was different from the other militaries in Latin America and after several months, I began to agree. The Honduran military was not elite. They were common folk with relatives in the lower middle and lower classes. They seemed to keep in touch with the masses. There were few shocking statistics about their behavior. They didn't do horrible things to their people because they were part of the people.

The generals took turns in ruling. Sometimes it was one person, sometimes it was a junta. But they never kept the reins very long. After a few years, the military would change leadership and other military personnel would surface. Although there were many civilians in the governmental structure, the top decision maker was a military man. And that was the type of government the younger Hondurans had always known.

The country was one of the poorest in the hemisphere, with only Haiti and Bolivia being more impoverished. Even though there were rich Hondurans and many Hondurans in the middle class, the majority were rural, almost illiterate, and extremely poor. The masses did not have much hope but all were allowed to speak their minds, seemingly without repercussions.

Honduras was the only Central American country bordering three other countries. It also had two coastlines. This made it very strategic property. While being pulled and tugged from all sides, Honduras remained friendly with the United States. There had never been a major confrontation between the two countries and in fact, the United States gave Honduras financial aid when natural disasters hit. There were no "gringo go home" signs anywhere. I could feel it was going to be a good place to work. There was lots to do from my perspective.

Since we were already comfortable with each other, the president's first words at the credentials ceremony were, "Well, how do you feel?"

I replied, "I'm delighted to be in Honduras but, to be honest, scared silly at the moment."

He said, "No se apene [not to worry], pretty soon all the reporters and photographers will leave and we can really chat." He thought I was just scared of the media. He had no idea I was scared of the whole thing. But I didn't correct his assumption and we continued with polite conversation and a few refreshments. After presenting him with my papers that stated that I was President Carter's personal envoy, I signed another document offered by the president stating that I was most welcome by Honduras to be the representative of the president of the United States, and the ceremony was all over. In a matter of minutes, all the months of preparation had come together.

Back to the official residence we went with the same fanfare, the crossed swords of the palace guards, and the parade of cars and escorts with the high-pitched sirens, to a champagne and finger food reception for everyone who had been involved. It was my first official party and while it was vivid at the time, it would eventually fade into a dim memory as all kinds of parties would begin to pile up in all the corners of my mind. As the ambassador, I would spend the next three years promoting human rights and striving to help Honduras on the road to democracy where everyone could participate. Everyone should have the same expectation of the good life. A home, good health, and of course, a good education should be expected by all, not just those born into a better existence.

Honduras was a country that had been ruled by military dictators for most of its history, although occasionally civilians would be allowed to rule and have power. When it was to the military's benefit, the civilians were ousted. The State Department had told me, "Your job is to go out there and help bring about a democracy." I would assist in giving birth to a democracy! And how does one do that when the country has been ruled by the military? Slowly and easily, with lots of faith; that's the only way to go.

Accepting invitations for parties and private evenings with influential individuals became an everyday event. After a day at the office, I would go home and exchange my business suit for an evening gown and high heels and go out again. It didn't take long for those high heels to cause a plantar wart on the bottom of my foot which took many months after my return home to finally get rid of. Every day was a twelve- to fourteen-hour day full of some kind of interesting activity, and I thrived on each and every one of them. Lucky for me, I needed little sleep and I was as healthy as a horse.

I accepted as many invitations as I could fit into my schedule and after each event, spent several hours writing reports to Washington on the results. While many think that ambassadors do nothing but attend and give parties, they don't realize that sometimes it is at social events that the real work is done and where skills are needed. Evenings were for making friends for our country. They were also an informal classroom. The Hondurans would learn about Americans by my example and in turn, I would learn about them. With so many expectations placed on me for exemplary behavior, the pressure was always on. I could never be seen with my hair down. I lived within imaginary glass walls where everyone could see me at any given moment and unseen bars, which made me feel rather hampered, but which were for my own safety.

It didn't take long for the Honduran military to say that I knew more about what was happening than they did! That was quite a compliment. I never thought my childhood was one of advantage, but it turned out to be. The Hondurans were able to sense that I was not an upper-class, rich American who came only in the name of self-gratification and glory. They could see it in the face of my Chicano farmer hanging in the entryway of the residence. They could read in me that I was not there to judge them, but to help them by making my country understand them. So they gave their friendship to me easily. I was unaware that I was fine-tuning my people skills and my new friends volunteered news freely because they felt I was *simpática* (empathetic). They knew I would help if I could and I, in turn, never abused their friendship. Rather, I used our relationship to further the cause of human rights. I would initiate conversations that might have been turned away coming from someone else as being a put-down. But with me, they knew my heart was good and I was concerned with the well-being of all humanity and they listened to what I had to say.

My friendships extended beyond just the government officials and other influential people of Honduras. One of my favorite groups of people happened to be one of the units of the embassy. It was the Peace Corps. Those volunteers were the best our country had to offer. They gave of themselves, not because of what they got paid, which was almost nothing, but because they believed so strongly in sharing their skills and talents and helping mankind's quality of life. These individuals were always very careful not to become too close to the American embassy. They didn't want anyone to think that they were with an intelligence agency. Because of the modesty and unselfishness they demonstrated, everywhere I went in the rural areas, I inquired if Peace Corps members were there so I could call attention and showcase their work and personally congratulate them.

I established a standing invitation at the residence for those members of the Peace Corps that lived in rural areas and happened to be in town. Any time it was available, they could swim at the residence. I had a lot of takers. It didn't take long for talk to begin among the staff that the Peace Corps volunteers would swim and use the pool house to do their laundry, drying their clothes on the lawn chairs that were placed around the pool. I gently but persuasively told the staff to allow them to do their laundry. I most certainly was not going to deny these unselfish people any small comfort I could provide them with. They were left alone after that and no comments were made regarding their use of the facilities.

I always saved slots at functions being held at the embassy and residence for them to attend if possible. And I, in turn, was always invited to all their functions, including a good old-fashioned Thanksgiving. I went to as many ceremonies, swearing-ins, good-byes, and other activities as I could and when I returned to the States, I made it a point to always stop and say hello at any Peace Corps office I might run across.

The majority of the Peace Corps volunteers in Honduras were assigned to the Ministry of Natural Resources. They helped dig wells and build pipelines and roads. They built schools and helped people start small businesses. They trained people to embroider, boil water, and care for children. They did anything that needed doing. Their lives were not glamorous at all. Many lived in shacks in the middle of nowhere, and many were young kids that could have been in the States going to universities, enjoying middle-class America with cars and frat parties. But these young people, as well as the several retirees who volunteered, took care of those whose knowledge and circumstances were less than their own. With very limited funding, they were the best ambassadors our country has ever had.

I have always been "results" oriented. My success at the end of each day was measured by what I had accomplished, not by what long hours I had worked. I delegated and organized until the cows came home. But despite my intensity at my job, I surprised many of my staff at the beginning because of my informality. I learned all their names and the names of many of their family members. I was aware of their personal problems and helped if I could, even if it was no more than a hug and a word of comfort or encouragement. They realized that I did not hold myself apart from them as ambassadors are rumored to do, and they soon became used to this new treatment. Outside the embassy, I was very careful to remain as formal as I needed to be with the Hondurans. They are more formal than Americans. But as they got to know me, I was able to make them as comfortable and relaxed with me as my other friends. I treated everyone the same whether that person was an ambassador or the old woman that sold fruit on a corner near the residence. She was ancient looking with white hair and had laid claim to a corner near the residence as her own for selling fruit. Every day as I left the residence to go to the embassy, I would wave at her as we passed by. She never returned the wave with any kind of gesture and I liked to think it was because the windows were tinted too dark for her to see me. Although I had been continually cautioned against giving money to the poor, on Christmas day one year, as I was leaving the residence to attend a party, there she was on the corner trying to sell her fruit. I thought to myself, I have been told "do this," "don't do that" and have followed all instructions to the letter! I live in a palace surrounded by bars! Just this once, I'm going to do what I want. I had the driver pull over and I got out and asked the *viejita*, "If I buy all your fruit, will it enable you to go home and spend this Christmas day with your family?"

She replied, "Señora, I would like you to buy all my fruit, but I will not go home to my family. Rather, I will go and buy more fruit so I can come back and sell it too." I was disappointed that my attempt at goodwill would not convince her to go home on Christmas, but I bought the fruit anyway because I was impressed with her honesty and drove on feeling that I had done something of a good deed.

As anyone in public life knows, reporters can be very difficult to contend with. The media is known the world over as heartless, pushy, and always looking for the worst dirt they can find on everybody. But the Honduran reporters were very kind to me. My very first press conference with them was probably a surprise to them but a completely natural thing for me to do. I'm a team builder and whether I'm working with kindergarten students or senior citizens, I believe that in order to get real participation, we have to sit in a circle if at all possible.

A week after having arrived, my deputy said the reporters were waiting for me in the conference room. I had spent a few days memorizing their names from pictures ahead of time, but as I walked in, I realized I would have to tell the staff the next time about how I would like to have the room prepared. Today there was a table at the front of the room and all the reporters were sitting in neat, orderly rows. As I greeted them, I told them I needed their help immediately. They were to stand up and help me put the chairs in a circle. Without delay, a wonderful dialogue started as we all moved chairs, including me. I am convinced that was the beginning of a wonderful friendship between us. We were equals, sharing what was close to our hearts.

My Spanish in the beginning did not always express what I wanted it to, but when it would be read in the newspaper, the reporters would have put the words in correctly for me. My reporter friends were also considerate when they wrote about other activities I was involved in. While I know I have large feet, they didn't mention their size when I got bitten on the toe by a bug. I had been at a reception in San Pedro Sula and had no idea how the culprit got into my shoe to perform its dastardly deed, but by the time I arrived home, my toe was so swollen that I couldn't wear shoes. The next day, I worked at the embassy without my usual high heels and by the following day in the paper, a headline read, "A la Señora Embajadora le pica una araña peluda." In English the headline meant "Madame Ambassador gets bitten by a hairy spider." The reporters were wonderful. At least they didn't tell the public I was running around barefoot and had size eight feet! And when the hammock I was relaxing on swinging under two trees one afternoon at home came untied and I fell to the ground on my derrière, no one made mention of it in the gossip column the next day. They thought I was their special friend, and in turn, they were definitely mine. I knew many of them by name and since the embassy and residence were normally off limits to the media, I had special socials just for them.

General Castro's reign had ended a year after I arrived in the country. He had not been able to cultivate the support of the larger landowners and that was how the military kept its power base. Before it happened, I was visited officially by a military group and told of the upcoming change. I felt sorry for the Castros, whom I had come to greatly admire and respect.

The three-man junta that took over power continued a close, professional relationship with me also. The junta was composed of the chief of the armed forces, General Paz Garcia; the head of the security forces, General Amílcar Zelaya; and the commander of the air force, General Álvarez Martínez.

General Paz was the head and the junta's voice became one of returning rule to civilians as soon as possible. About a year into their rule, civilians were encouraged to choose representatives for their new congress. Their sole job was to set up an interim government and create the procedures for the upcoming elections to be held the following year. General Paz was named the interim president and a civilian, Suazo Córdova, was named the president of the congress.

By 1981, they were ready for elections for both the president and the congress. The elections were held without a hitch and Suazo Córdova was elected president. The decade-long military rule had ended. But just as important during this time, the Hondurans had avoided bloodshed, which was just the opposite of all their neighboring countries.

The president that came to power after the junta was General Paz García. He had gotten there partly due to the short war, the Soccer War, between Honduras and El Salvador. The two countries had been angry with each other for some time because of a boundary dispute and the movement of many Salvadorans into Honduran territory. The actual fighting had started after a soccer game. General García was a hero during that war and now he had become president.

When the head of state from a foreign country goes to the United States, the U.S. ambassador of that country is expected to go. For me, these trips were very educational and I had opportunities to see many wonderful things. Once, General García took me to West Point with him. American soldiers were at attention wherever we went. On this particular trip, there was a helicopter being made for him. General Alexander Haig was the CEO of the company.

President García and his entourage went to the Waldorf Astoria in New York because he was addressing the Council of the Americas while on this particular trip. We had checked in with four young photographers who had come with us from Honduras. Fifteen minutes later, all their equipment was stolen. Despite my efforts to get them reimbursed through the hotel and our State Department, it was to no avail. No one would help. I was never so embarrassed in my life! Imagine the impression those young men had of our country. They had warned me about thieves in Honduran streets; I should have warned them about ours.

I began to put a name to the skills I had learned as a child. It was no longer just a matter of a sympathetic student helping out a fellow student with answers. That had been the beginning steps of politics for me. I began to understand not only diplomacy, but international diplomacy. One seldom spoke directly and I was a master of that already from my civil rights work. Situations arose almost daily in which I had to tell racists that they were racists without using those words. Their beliefs were hurting children and I couldn't allow that. I tried to help them realize that they had an awareness that was buried inside their subconscious. They needed to find these natural, innate convictions and define them. I reminded them of these moral convictions every chance I got and saw them begin to surface as these individuals began to recognize what they were feeling inside but didn't understand from years of dictatorship.

Countries with coastlines have many natural disasters such as hurricanes and occasional earthquakes. Honduras is no different. As ambassador, it was a given that I should offer financial support to help resolve problems that arose from these disasters. I had an emergency fund available at my fingertips. This fund was one I could use immediately rather than having to go through all the red tape of writing a proposal, having it reviewed, accepted, or revised, and on and on and on.

When the first hurricane hit the Mosquitia coastal area after I had become ambassador, I didn't even feel a slight breeze, living inland as I did. But as I flew over the areas that were hit in a helicopter with several Honduran officials, I couldn't stop the tears that ran freely down my face. Below me was a scene of total devastation. I felt so sad that I couldn't do more than I was able. Houses which were made from any material they could find to serve as walls to support the lightweight thatched roofs were completely leveled. Roads had disappeared and family garden plots that were needed for food were thoroughly destroyed. But the worst thing was the lack of clean drinking water. People in these rural areas had no processing plants to purify their water. Instead, they used wells, streams, and ditches. The hurricane had completely polluted all their water. Salty ocean water had washed over ditches and stream banks, either breaking them or filling them with undrinkable water. Wells were no longer usable and new ones would have to be dug. In addition, these people who had just lost everything they owned didn't even have shelter to protect them at night when the mosquitoes were out in full force.

As soon as I returned to the embassy, I initiated the work related to setting up a tent city for those left homeless and had fresh water flown into them while additional monies were sought for help. This would not be the last time in my three years that I would deal with devastation of this nature. I viewed disaster areas where mudslides and hurricanes had hit or even where rough seas had damaged the countryside.

The revolution in Nicaragua was another long-lasting "emergency." The Sandinistas had fought the repressive Somoza regime in a protracted battle that had killed many Nicaraguans. Many Hondurans were sympathetic to the cause because they had seen and heard about the brutality of the military in the next-door country. At the beginning of the war, as people started moving across the border to escape the killing, Honduran citizens helped by giving them places to stay.

But as the battles intensified and Nicaraguans crossed the border in ever-increasing numbers, it became too much for the few "safe houses" and the excess people became a big problem for the Honduran government. The need for clean water, tent cities, food, and all kinds of health requirements, became an overpowering burden. It was too much to ask Honduras, a poor country itself, to do much more. I was able to help with my emergency funds, but never enough to really make a dent in the horrendous problem.

By the time victory for the Sandinistas was declared, Honduras had made a tremendous sacrifice to try to help these displaced neighbors. Although not all Hondurans believed in Sandinismo, all agreed that the refugee situation was a humanitarian problem of gigantic proportions for a small country like Honduras.

Indirectly, I continued visiting and encouraging the poor in Honduras, the peasants in the fields and banana plantations. When an old lady was trembling during one of my personal visits, I put my arm around her in a comforting gesture just as I would back home in my own special way of defying the negative and cruel stigmas attached to poverty-stricken people, and asked, "Why are you trembling?" She answered, "I'm so scared to talk to you. You're the American ambassador."

I said, "My president sent me to talk to all the people of Honduras. You need not be afraid. We all have basic human rights and you need to be able to talk about yours." I gave her a lesson right then and there. She was just like the little old man in my picture that was my social conscience. I loved her on the spot and held her in my arms until she calmed down.

Sometimes, protocol created a problem for me. I didn't know all the "ins" and "outs" related to that mysterious science. People wanted to sit next to me wherever I went. Once after having gone through the buffet line at an affair held in an affluent private home, I took a seat on the nearest sofa expecting, as always, for others to join me. But tonight, no one would sit next to me on this huge sofa. Wondering what was wrong, my internal voice said, I used Scope and took a bath, so why won't anyone sit with me? After a short time, an embassy officer came and whispered in my ear, "Madame Ambassador, you're sitting on the wrong end of the sofa." Where I was sitting, everyone would be on the right and therefore appear more important than I. I thought because of protocol, things got done, but at the same time, it got in the way of getting things done. So I experimented to see if this couch thing worked. I stood up and nonchalantly studied a picture hanging on the wall and because I stood there for so long pondering my next move, I have always remembered the peaceful pastoral scene and the rich gold-leaf frame. After feeling I had been standing long enough, I returned to sit on the opposite side of the sofa. Then the people joined me in droves! It was funny to me, but a dead serious matter in the diplomatic world. Real issues were more important to me and that's what I had spent my time studying when I had gotten my briefings in Washington, and that's what I wanted to do now, but I knew protocol was my constant companion like my body guards.

I had been asked to attend the seminars given to ambassadors' wives on art and protocol. But I wasn't a wife, I was an ambassador, so I had refused to do it because I did not want to take time from my high-powered briefings. I therefore created my own art for the residence and embassy children's drawings became my masterpieces. Plants created the color. Calendar pictures filled up other empty spaces. It wasn't until the last year that I was in Honduras that I was sent many beautiful art pieces from Washington. But they still didn't replace the art of the children nor the old man on the adobe wall that hung in my entrance for all to see.

So went the next three years. They sped by. On a daily basis at 7:30 in the morning, I would meet with my country team, all the heads of the different divisions. At night, I put on my evening dresses and high heels and really went to do some very important work for my country.

American Embassy, Tegucigalpa, Honduras, 1979

Taking the oath of office as first Mexican American woman ambassador, as my husband and Warren Christopher look on, September 1977

Presenting credentials in Honduras, October 1977

Presenting credentials to the president, General Melgar Castro, October 1977

Sharing a light moment with the university women of Tegucigalpa, Honduras, September 1978

127

With prospective students, El Mochito, Honduras, 1978

Presented with a lovely gift, El Progreso, Honduras, 1978

Exploring a coffee farm, Danlí. Honduras, 1978

Greeting townspeople, Valle de Ángeles, Honduras, 1979

Greeted at the outskirts of town by the people of Ojojona, 1980

With the U. S. Marines and the cake of cakes, Tegucigalpa, Honduras, 1979

Greeting President Carter outside the White House, March 1980

131

Visiting a Peace Corps volunteer, Puerto Lempira, Honduras, 1980

Farewell. Presented the highest honor given to foreigners, September 1980

Not the Same Little Mexican

The ceremony at the end of my tour of duty to honor me that brought on rivers of tears took place in a huge warehouse in the northern part of the country. Most work had been stopped at nearby plantations and farms so the laborers could attend. There were very few occasions when these operations stopped work and I was astounded that it had been done for a simple shoemaker's daughter from Las Vegas, New Mexico. The majority were members of labor unions. Droves of ordinary people came from everywhere that day. Some of them arrived riding horses, some came in trucks, and others walked. They all had one thing in common. They were the hard-working poor. Some of them were illiterate, but they all were the ones that were so often forgotten, and the ones that I had spoken out for the hardest.

Anyone who wanted to get up and speak was allowed. The presentations of flowers, clay pots, plaques, and other homemade items along with the beautiful things that were said about me as an American who loved the laborers had me crying until the tears rolled down my face. The ceremony lasted more than two hours and when it was over, the labor specialist from the embassy whispered to me, "This is a first, Madame Ambassador. Never has an American ambassador been honored by the labor unions of a foreign country in this manner. This has been an unbelievable experience."

When it was my turn to get up and speak, I had composed myself enough to more or less speak coherently and thank them, but I couldn't stop the tears. I was finally adjusted to speaking in public and my knees hadn't shaken in a long time, but today I couldn't control them. I was so filled with emotion that I could say nothing more than, "Thank you. You are the backbone of your country. You are the ones that keep it going. Keep working hard and always strive for the quality of life you are entitled to. Make sure to work for the basic necessities for everyone." I know I said more, but I was overwhelmed at the time and couldn't recall later what it was.

I looked for the old woman I had talked to on one of my tours, realizing that it would probably be next to impossible to find her if she had come. But she had touched my heart and I would always remember her. She had such a weather-beaten face, creased with deep wrinkles from years of working in the sun. Her straw hat looked almost as old as she and her clothes were rough and dirty. When I talked to her that day, I had, by then, really spread my wings. I gave her a hug and I could see in the background several *viejitos*. Thinking one of them might be her husband, I imagined him ready to lecture her after I left that she shouldn't have dared to talk to me. But it was part of my calling to talk to everyone I met and provide the opportunity to discuss human rights. She was as important to me as anyone else.

The banana plantations were mazes and quite amazing. There were rows of huge banana trees with *racimos*, the large banana clusters. There were also thick conveyor belts or cables strung between the rows. These belts were for hanging the banana *racimos* after they had been picked off the trees. They would somehow slide down between the rows to the processing areas. Here there were long metal tubs filled with water where the bunches of bananas would float through the processes of being washed, separated by size, and selected for quality for export. The best bananas were saved for Hondurans. This was easy because the tastiest bananas are the small ones and ironically enough, Americans prefer the large ones which really have a flavor as flat as paper compared to their smaller brothers. The *viejita* had worked in a nearby area where the new banana plants were growing and her labor was intensive for someone as tired as she.

When I read the paper the next morning after this particular ceremony, I wasn't prepared for the headline: "The American ambassador has cried for Hondurans, and Hondurans have cried for her." It was only one of several articles that had been written about me when my tour of duty was almost over. Another article said there was no doubt in people's minds that if I ran for president, I would win. I was embarrassed by that one. I wondered what President García was thinking. My reporter friends had succeeded in bringing tears to my eyes more than once with their compliments. This outpouring of human feeling touched me more than any other event in my life.

It became a time when I looked upon myself as having done a good job. I had achieved what I had set out to do. For the first time in my life, I wasn't criticizing myself and saying, Mari-Luci, you didn't do a good enough job. I felt satisfied and wouldn't have changed anything if I had it to do over. I had given it my best! I was proud of my efforts.

It was a mixed blessing for me that it was now time to go home. Even though I had been expecting to act as ambassador for only perhaps a year or a year and a half, I wasn't notified by the State Department that my tour of duty was up until three years later. By this time, Honduras was busy writing the legal documents to conduct free elections. They had become very active with political parties. Not only were the politicians involved, but the common folk as well. There was an underlying excitement and belief that it was possible they were going to become a real democracy. Even the young students who had only known dictatorship since birth dared to believe.

During my last six weeks in Honduras, I was wined and dined unbelievably by every sector of Honduran society. There were government functions at which all the different ministers and my colleagues at the embassy said goodbye. The official government farewell was quite an honor. They gave me the medal of Francisco Morazán. This man is a Honduran hero. He tried to unify Central America in the nineteenth century. He left a legacy of establishing habeas corpus and trial by jury. He worked to have all religions accepted. He can also perhaps be given credit for the two party systems in Central America. While I was no Francisco Morazán, I felt good that I had played a small part in starting to help free this country from the chains of dictatorship, poverty, and illiteracy. This medallion is given only to those who strengthen the links in the chain that binds two countries together, and they had given one to me!

I am still asked how I was able to accomplish such a monumental task in a country whose government was such a contrast to ours. My standard answer is that I helped it along with diplomacy, using skills I was fortunate enough to learn while growing up in a home rich in Hispanic tradition. Though I had not known the words used to label these skills as a child, today they have become defined and refined. I was a master of diplomacy, negotiating and bartering. My respect for the common people and my treatment of them as equals had come naturally even in childhood, and I had no need for words to label my empathy. Respect and compassion was something I tried to teach others by demonstrating these qualities every day of my life. We were equal partners on the road of life.

The night I accepted the Francisco Morazán Medal, I wore a special black chiffon gown that had been especially made for me. The fabric had large but delicately painted pastel flowers on it. It was new for the occasion and held an emotional significance for me. The fabric had been a gift from a close Honduran friend who had brought it from Rome, Italy. The gesture was reminiscent of the peach-colored chiffon dress given to me by my baker friend so long ago who had also brought hers back from Rome. Another beautiful dress for another prominent night was made for me from that material when I was only the second member of my family to graduate from the eighth grade.

I was also given the Dual Citizen Award by the governor of Tegucigalpa, making me an honorary citizen of Honduras. But on this and other occasions, I wore gowns that had been seen before. I still amazed myself with the size of the wardrobe I had acquired. I felt so extravagant after growing up in flour-sack dresses. But even with all the clothes I had bought during my ambassadorship, I never filled the closets in my dressing room at the residence. It was about twenty-eight feet wide with two bathrooms and closet space galore. It was lined with drawer after drawer for undergarments and shelf after shelf meant for shoes. There were lots of bright lights around a gigantic mirror, enabling me to put on my makeup and knowing it was always just right.

The luxuries didn't end there. The staff that took care of Heri and me in our personal quarters went so far as to clean our toothbrushes with boiling water every day after we had used them. I had never been catered to in all my life. I did, however, finally draw the line when they tried to iron my pantyhose. That was just going too far. It was hard to ask them to stop and not hurt their feelings, but I just couldn't imagine myself walking around with creases down the fronts of my hose.

Many personal friends, both Honduran and American, that I made during my stay held dinners, luncheons, and breakfasts for me. And in between all those meals, I squeezed in coffees and teas because there was just no way to fit in all the invitations. I was so busy with these functions that when the day came to finally leave for the States, three years to the day that I had arrived in Honduras, it came suddenly. Hugs and kisses from staff saw us off when we left for the airport. This time though, when I got to the airport, I understood about first class and the use of the VIP lounge. Many Honduran citizens and reporters were there to bid me farewell as a friend. Embassy personnel were there also to see me off with tears and good wishes. I loved them all.

Heri and I got on the plane and we were so filled with emotion that the only words he could say to me were, "Well, you did it!" I could only reply with, "We did it!" so that I wouldn't begin to cry all over again.

The plane took off and we were on our way to Washington where I had been told I would become the Deputy Assistant Secretary of State for Latin America. But what I was really going back for was to be trained to become an ambassador to another Latin American country. However, when I got there, because there were upcoming elections, it was decided to delay my training for the second country. So I put my whole heart and soul into becoming a good deputy assistant secretary.

Coming back to Washington, we had moved into an apartment not far from the State Department that belonged to a Honduran friend. We had taken very little with us while at the residence in Honduras, so everything was in storage and we had few of our personal things. Being so much like my mom, feeling the need to create a homey atmosphere and make everything pretty and nice, I improvised and quickly made some decorations to make the apartment more homey. I took tree branches and stuck them in pots with yellow crepe paper flowers glued on them. I called these forsythia, and placed them in front of mirrors and other areas. Every can I opened became a pot for clippings of plants. Flowers were fairly inexpensive and we treated ourselves to fresh flowers, consistently reminding us of the Honduran residence.

We had sold our car in Honduras and it took awhile for the new Mercedes Benz we had ordered from Germany to arrive, so I became a user of the bus system. I had never walked the streets or used public transportation in any large city in my entire life and every day became an adventure. I loved riding the bus even though as the weather changed from warm to rainy and snowy, cars and buses passing by occasionally splashed slush on my coat and legs. I began to notice the homeless sitting on the grates to stay warm and tried to establish eye contact with them to strike up a sort of friendship.

One particular man was such a fixture that when he passed away, there was an article about him in the paper. He had strikingly beautiful white hair but was so unkempt that I made a wide circle around him as I passed because of his strong smell. He scared me and I stopped attempting to make eye contact with him. I just prayed to the Blessed Mother to take care of him.

As I walked the streets from the bus stop to the State Department, I noticed that there were always coins that had dropped from people's pockets while they were putting money into the parking meters and I began picking them up and giving them to the homeless. It would later become a challenge between my brother-in-law and me to see who could pick up the most coins during the year. Whoever was the winner would be treated to a nice dinner. I usually won and the total I picked up went to charity.

Once the car arrived, Heri took me to work every morning and picked me up every evening. He had been looking for a job everywhere and when it became clear that he wouldn't be able to find one, he became a connoisseur of the museums. He knew every museum in town and every weekend we would go together to one he hadn't seen. Washington, D.C., has so much to offer that we never ran out of things to experience and see.

I'm not one for playing the games of bureaucracy, so I had to modify my methods of communicating. In politics, it is an art to know what is not said but implied, what gets beaten around the bush, and how to act and not to act. I was learning my job well when our presidential elections were held. When Ronald Reagan won, I immediately knew that my time was up and I was no longer going to another country. I knew that we should return home. However, Heri wanted to stay and continue to try to find a job. I kept saying, "We need to go home." There was a feeling that had begun to grow inside me calling me home. But Heri wanted to stay, so ever the good wife, I agreed to remain awhile longer.

I could see the handwriting on the wall that everybody from Carter's administration was jumping ship. Several people told me, "Stay here. Soon the euphoria will dissipate and you will be sent as ambassador to the other country." Meanwhile, Republican friends were working very hard to get me to stay, but the attitude at the capital was "sweep the Democrats out of town."

I declined to stay. It was not in me to represent the new president's philosophy. His policies were not something I could wrap my arms around as I had the human rights promoted by Jimmy Carter. President Reagan wanted to concentrate on economic development and lesser government. "Let the poor get out and work and reduce welfare" was heard all over the capital. President Reagan wanted to build up the military and Starwars, all the kinds of things that I questioned so much.

After a memorandum came down from the president stating that he would not read anything longer than a one-page memo regardless of the topic, I thought to myself, "Wow! I can't stay here one day more. I gotta go home." I began to pressure Heri in earnest that we needed to finally announce that I was going home.

He soon realized that I was very unhappy and a few days later agreed and said, "OK, let's go home."

So, after thanking everyone profusely, I said, "Thank you for wanting me to stay, but no thank you." I came in the front door and would leave through the front door.

After the decision to go home, I immediately called the president at the University of New Mexico and asked if he could find me a job for the summer. I wanted him to be the first to know even before I called the dean in my college. He told me, "You come home immediately. I have a job for you no matter what day it is that you walk into my office." So Heri and I prepared to return home.

We began to deal with all the logistics of going home. Our house had been leased and there were many other things to think about. When paperwork and other things were finally completed, we left for the land of enchantment. We packed everything we owned in our new Mercedes, including a nine-dollar artificial silk hyacinth with three blossoms that I had bought when decorating the apartment. It was the only thing that wouldn't fit into any crevices in the car, so I rode the whole way home with it between my feet where it wouldn't bother either of us.

When we left the capital, we didn't realize how uptight we had been until we reached the first rest stop. After walking around for a while, when we got back in the car, we couldn't start it. Minutes later, somebody pulled up at the rest stop and offered to help. He got in and started it immediately. We had been so stressed and worn out that we didn't remember the car had to be in neutral to start. I prayed the rest of the way home and nothing else happened on the way.

When we got to Albuquerque, my sister and brother-in-law invited us to stay with them. We appreciated their offer because it was difficult to come home with everything so displaced. We stayed a couple of weeks while negotiating with the professor who had leased our house to move out. We convinced her and spent much time helping her pack so we could move in more quickly.

We had bought our home in Albuquerque while we were in Honduras. It was a beautiful adobe building complete with stained-glass windows. It had adobe *bancos* everywhere, along with three fireplaces. There was also a wood-burning stove in the den that gave off the kind of heat that warmed you all the way to your soul. All the adobe brick was exposed on the inside and open around the atrium, which quickly became the garden room. Upon arriving home, we painted and did other things to make it clean and ours again.

Following the president of the university's advice, I immediately went to his office to say hello. I was named assistant to the president that same day. That was a fun job because I represented the university president in places where he didn't want to go. I loved it. But the best thing he did for me was to have me go to the library and talk to people in order to become reacquainted with U.S. society.

At the beginning when he offered that, I thought it was odd, but I realized quickly how important that was. I didn't know more than just the headlines in the paper about what had taken place in the United States for the past three years. Much had happened to our society while we were gone. I had left a Chicana and when I returned we had become Hispanic Americans. None of my close friends were smoking anymore. Feminists were burning their bras and opening their own doors. You don't notice changes taking place when you are a part of them, but if you go away and come back, you see the changes. Being a traditional Chicana, I needed time to read and reflect and become reacquainted with our progressing country.

Within a few months of our return to New Mexico, I was named the director of SHRI (Southwest Hispanic Research Institute). The institute was to study Hispanic issues. I loved that job too! It was in its first fledgling steps. Administrative details were still being worked out. The professionals involved weren't really sure where it was to be housed or even whom to report to. I met wonderful people who were really interested in the cause of researching Hispanic issues and concerns.

During my time in civil rights, the general attitude was best expressed by the phrases "Let's do something" and "Try to show what can be done in education." But we really didn't have in-depth research on how issues affected the Hispanic community. So when I returned to the university and this effort was in place, I was in awe. That was what we had needed all along.

With my exciting new position, I was once again invited to speak across the country. In fact, I spoke more than I ever had before. But while I was speaking strictly on civil rights, now I was invited to speak at conferences because I was "Madame Ambassador." I enjoyed that part but had to get used to writing my own speeches again. I still spoke about Hispanic issues, but I spoke also about what I had done as an ambassador and how others could prepare themselves to do the same.

What bothered Mari-Luci, the person, most during this time was being treated with deference. With the title of ambassador, how could I still be the same person I was before? I hadn't expected that. People were doing slightly different things. I picked up on it right away and was very uncomfortable with it. I had wanted to go back and crawl into my little comfort hole again. But the more people treated me differently, the more I realized, "Mari-Luci, you aren't the same person that left. You are different. You have undergone some personal changes. You're still shy, but now you can speak. You're still shy, but now you're not afraid to act on policy."

It seemed to me that I had begun to look at the world and society in different ways. My vision of the world had opened up tremendously. All those years of traveling in Latin America had transformed me into a citizen of the world with an extraordinary vision of global happenings. I knew the other side of the fence and how Latin Americans view us. This gave me knowledge to use here in the States. I now understood the problems in other countries, which facilitated my global thinking. I clearly saw that education was not enough. There had to be a change of attitude in the upper and middle classes for the poor to advance as a group in any country. Otherwise, it wouldn't happen.

Some close friends told me that something inside me had changed. On a personal level, I was the same, but I had a much bigger vision and was much more open minded. No longer was my thinking limited to one geographical location. Professionally, I had grown tremendously. Personally, I had refined my personal and political views much more. Previously, I couldn't talk about them, but now I knew what "global" meant. One night I confided to a close friend that I was no longer "the same little Mexican" who had left town. I now spoke with authority and conviction when my ethnic group was demeaned.

I had succeeded in penetrating the male-dominated world. I was the only woman at most of the meetings while ambassador, whether it was in the United States or Honduras. Exciting topics ranged from Cuba to drugs to military policy and on and on. I became so accustomed to being the only woman that when other women appeared I thought, Hurray for you! How wonderful to see another woman empowered. Today, at least half of any group are women.

Heri got a job at UNM similar to the one he had before we left and we quickly fell back into our old routine. The only thing different this time was that my mom came to live with us. My sister and brother-in-law had taken care of her since they had picked her up that day from her porch where she was waiting for them. It was my turn now. I looked forward to Mom's company. Mom continued to tell me stories of her childhood which would still enrich my life, even now. I was able to enjoy my mother's company but my children were engrossed in their studies and at the beginning of their professions and family life. I would see them from time to time and we would catch up on all the news, but Mom was my continuing companion.

We were very happy and thought our lives would be normal from then on. We had been back almost six years when I started being courted by the Educational Testing Service (ETS). One of the vice presidents called me and said ETS needed an assistant vice president. My name had surfaced and the director was hoping I would be interested. I had learned never to close a door and said, "Sure, I'm interested." The vice president, who happened to be a woman, flew in from Princeton, New Jersey, to interview me. She determined that I would be a perfect fit. My assignment would be to head a satellite office in Oakland, California, and work with the California legislature. It was this last thing that really hooked me. I had learned to love politics and looked forward to becoming involved at a new level. Heri and I talked back and forth about the invitation and decided this was a tremendous opportunity that we must not let pass. It paid much more than what I earned at UNM. I was close to "early" retirement, so I could take it with less pay, but I would make it up in actual cash while I worked. Once again we made a joint decision that this would be a good opportunity and off we went.

I knew legislative work would be fun. I would get to talk to legislators about testing and ask what the company could do for them. I would find out what kind of information ETS could provide for a better understanding of the issues related to testing. This was very important.

There are some people against testing in any way, shape, or form. Many minorities feel that testing affects them disproportionately. Most testing measures experiences that middle-class white kids have as opposed to the experiences of those who live in barrios and poor neighborhoods. Even the vocabulary used in the tests represents middle-class Anglo America. The tests are not based on what one learns and memorizes in school, but the experiences acquired both before and during school. While I believe that minorities are affected by the use of tests, those tests tell us that minorities haven't had those types of experiences. So the issue becomes one of how we could fight the system so we could have those experiences for our people. I wanted minorities to have a voice to ensure that they will not be left out because they haven't had the experiences that middle-class kids have.

When I began my actual work with ETS, it was fun to introduce myself as a new arrival. Now experienced in meeting strangers, I felt only confidence. I found that nearly everyone I went to visit was appreciative of my coming. They almost always offered to help with any information our company needed.

Several legislators were amenable to testing. One in particular that I became friendly with told me that he would love to introduce me to the legislature when they were in session. I knew it was because of my title of ambassador and it made me smile inside. That was a highlight for me and very satisfying because I had little name recognition in California.

From those beginning steps in the capital walking the halls and introducing myself, becoming friends with secretaries so I could get to see the assemblypersons and senators when I needed to; I became sure of myself and of what I needed to do. Willie Brown was the president of the legislature and one day I introduced myself to him. Somehow we seemed to hit it off. I cannot claim him as a friend, but at the time there was something that sparked.

When there was an opening to join the commission of post-secondary education, lo and behold, Mr. Brown appointed me to that commission. People came up to me asking how I was named to that commission. I hadn't been in California even a year, and already I was on one of the most prestigious educational commissions in the state. I still kept feeling that I wasn't a politician. I remember saying, "I'm not a politician. What I am is a representative for a very powerful company. That's probably how I got the position."

I became directly involved with planning post-secondary education. I visited universities. I really got involved in the educational scene in California and enjoyed it immensely. I got reacquainted with a lot of people I had known at the universities and made many new friends. The many trips I made to Sacramento were taken with great affection. There were many nights when I was invited to events at the legislature. I would always go even though I would have to drive home on the lonely road by myself and still be at work at my usual six in the morning.

The one aspect of moving to California that was difficult was that my mother had become quite ill with hardening of the arteries. But it was my turn to take care of her, my sister having done so while we were in Honduras. She had brought Mom down from Las Vegas.

For a while, Mom had stayed completely alone in Las Vegas after Grandma died. My sister would call her constantly in an effort to convince her to come live with her in Albuquerque, but Mom absolutely refused. All of a sudden, one day she just went and sat on the front porch. She had been there so long that a neighbor who kept an eye on her went over and asked her what she was doing. Mom said she was waiting for Vera to come and pick her up because she was moving to Albuquerque. The neighbor rushed in and called my sister. She knew our mom would go through phases of forgetting things. Vera and her husband left immediately to go to Las Vegas to get her. By the time they got there a few hours later, she was still sitting in exactly the same spot.

Mom never went back. They brought her, leaving the house exactly as it was until the roof caved in, destroying most everything that had been left behind. Pictures of us as children were lost along with other mementos. It broke my heart when I had to have the house leveled when we returned because it was a danger in the neighborhood.

So Mom went with us even though she was seriously ill already. Heri went ahead and found a house that had a bedroom and bathroom on the first floor for her. I was excited in one sense to move because my brother lived nearby. He had been gone from New Mexico since he was seventeen years old. This became a great opportunity for us to become reacquainted and he would have an opportunity to see Mom often.

I started work right away and Heri once again was in a situation in which he was looking for work. He finally found a job at the University of the Pacific. It was a good job with the exception that he was traveling quite a bit. In the beginning he would try to come back every day, but the driving was hard on him. Next, he tried staying at the student dormitory three days a week. That didn't work, either, and finally he decided to get an apartment. He would leave Monday morning and come back Friday evening. That became a way of life for us and it began an insidious downhill spiral in our marriage that would become irreversible.

Meanwhile, my mother became sicker and sicker until the day finally came when Heri physically carried her to the car and we drove to the hospital. I sat in the backseat with her knowing in my heart that she wasn't coming back. She was in the hospital five days before she passed away. We stayed with her as much as we could. My brother and sister-in-law were there and on the third day, I called my sister in Albuquerque and told her, "Sis, if you're planning to come, why don't you come now?"

One of the nurses had told me, "You know, this woman is hanging on for some reason. Has she seen all her children?"

I said, "No, there's a daughter that's not here yet." I hadn't wanted to tell my sister, but that's what was on my mind. So I called my sister and brother-in-law and they came the next day. That was the fourth day and right away they went to visit her. We went home that night and when we got back the next morning, she was sitting up in bed. Heri began giving her breakfast, and I combed her hair, which she had kept long and traditional, and began fixing braids on her, putting big pink bows on the ends. All of a sudden, she sort of heaved and laid her head back on the pillow. She had spent the last seven years of her life with me and now she was gone.

Losing Mom was difficult for me. She had always been my best friend. I had identified with her completely and realized that I had become an exact replica of her, with the exception of having a professional career and going through a divorce.

We brought her back on a plane to Albuquerque to bury her. When the planes changed, I asked special permission and was able to go back to be with her as they moved her coffin to our connecting flight.

The day we buried her in Albuquerque it was cold and windy. Lots of friends came to pray the rosary and then came the next day for the funeral. It was a sad day for me. It took a long time to recover from her death. I couldn't even mention her name without starting to cry broken-heartedly for the terrible loss I felt.

For the first two months after her death, I wore black most of the time. I remember the first day I finally wore color. I wore a black suit and put a fuchsia tie on my white blouse. It was a sign that I was beginning to be able to let go of that horrible void in my life. I started working and adjusting a little more. But it took a year before I could talk about my mother. We had been so close.

It had also been difficult for me when Grandma passed away, but her death happened while I was in Honduras and I wasn't as close to the situation. She died of old age at ninety-six and unlike my mother, still had all her faculties. I cried and cried because we were very close. I felt terrible that I hadn't been with her at the end nor been able to attend her funeral. I just had a miserable time. I got over it much sooner, though, because I didn't see her. I was with strangers and had a terribly important job that was very public. It helped to repress my feelings.

My sister didn't call me until after she had been buried. She had made the decision that since I had only been there a few months, it was too soon for me to leave my new post. She knew I would have made every effort to get back.

When the embassy personnel heard about her death, they, along with several other friends, had masses read for her. We attended several masses in her honor. I went into my routine of private praying which I do a lot. It was hard knowing I would never see my Nanita again, but I had realized that when I said my good-byes to her when we left for Honduras, it would be the last time I would see her. But Grandma was very sweet and concerned about others' feelings, never talking about her own problems to the very end.

I had a couple of setbacks after my mom died. I was terribly lonely in our huge, empty house. Heri didn't really live there anymore. He only came on Saturdays and Sundays. I didn't like living alone, but couldn't say anything because he had been so long without a job. His job was very important to him, so I kept struggling with my loneliness silently.

It was getting closer and closer to the end of our marriage when the horrible earthquake of 1987 happened. I was in the big house and Heri was on his way home from work in Stockton. I had just gotten home, coming in from the garage through the laundry room and into the den. As I opened the door to the den,

I felt a swish of air inside. It was loud and I thought someone had broken in and left a shattered window. I was so afraid of living alone in that huge house that I just panicked. I started to withdraw and go back outside when the house started trembling. I knew I was in my first earthquake.

The house swayed back and forth. We had what was termed a "safe haven" under the stairwell and I began to make my way through the house in an effort to reach it. I ran from the den into the hall where the floor was moving in a wave, just like the ocean. All the pictures hanging on the wall were moving and I had the sensation that I was being banged from one side of the hall to the other as I was trying to advance to our safe haven under the stairway. As I got through the corridor, I could see the dining room chandelier, which hung on a long chain, swinging from one side of the room to the other, slamming into the wall on one side and the iron stair railing on the other. I had to walk under it to reach the other side and hesitated, uncertain as to whether the chandelier would come crashing down on my head if I attempted to cross the room.

Making a decision that took only a split second, I made it through the room and when I turned the corner, two Mexican silver fighting roosters came crashing down along with some violets on top of the china closet. I thought everything in the china closet would be lost, but as I finally reached the safe haven where the flashlight and emergency items were stored and reached out to turn the door handle, the earthquake stopped. It hadn't taken more than a few seconds. I opened the door to a sudden deafness after all the terrible noise. It had sounded like ocean waves.

I took a deep breath and looked out the living room window to see all the neighbors running into the street. Rather than joining them, I sat down on the living room sofa so I could relive the last few terrible moments and always remember them in every detail. I was sitting on the sofa reflecting and saying a prayer to El Santo Niño when Heri drove into the driveway. I ran down the corridor I had just been through and opened the den and laundry room door to reach him as he started to get out of the car. I asked him if he was OK. He looked at me strangely and said, "Of course. Why are all those people in the street?"

I said, "Heri, we've just had the worst earthquake that California has had in years." He hadn't heard, seen, or felt a thing.

Because there was a professional baseball game, everyone had been let out of work early, and that was the only thing that prevented even more death on the Oakland Bay Bridge when it collapsed. My office was five minutes away from the bridge and anything that wasn't bolted down in our offices had toppled over. Filing cabinets, papers, chairs, and many other items were all over the floor.

The earthquake magnified my situation. I had to travel to Princeton, New Jersey, to the home office almost monthly. I was traveling constantly to Sacramento, working in the legislature. I went down to the Pasadena office a lot. I was very busy, but at the same time, I was also fully responsible for this huge house, the lawns, and the gardening. Always alone, it got to be too much for me.

I had known there were a lot of things going wrong in our marriage. I'm not one to deny it. Living in separate homes made it more and more obvious to me that we had reached a time in our lives when we were losing all the things we had in common. I brought up some subjects that Heri and I differed on which offended him, but I stuck to my guns.

I told him one weekend, "Come hell or high water, we're going to resolve this problem." Well, he decided it would be hell and high water and we didn't resolve the problem. We argued and argued and neither of us would budge.

I said, "Look, if this is where we are, we might as well get a divorce." I was tired of fighting and being so alone. Heri was shocked that I would even mention it and was sure that I wouldn't go through with it. But I just felt that it was something I had to confront and now was the time.

For more than a year we didn't talk to each other, he often did not come home, and we argued and argued. Finally, the dam broke. I went to a lawyer and he went to a lawyer and the lawyers took us to town. We paid an unbelievable amount of money.

I'm not a confrontational person and this was a very hard time for me. Finally, after a year of disagreement, I threw in the towel and said, "Let it be done."

My lawyer said, "No. You've got to stick it out."

I said, "I won't. I won't spend another day arguing. Just close this. Whatever happens, happens." My lawyer was very disappointed in me, but closed it off. Several months and thousands of dollars after that I decided it was time to address the issues we had disagreed on, and it was finally over. I was divorced and really alone once again.

As quickly as I could, I moved out of that huge home and into a condo right by my office. I could even walk if I wanted to. I began getting over all the pain and hurt of the past year. Moving to an apartment had helped a lot.

For months, we didn't talk except through our lawyers. There were many loose ends that just seemed to go on and on. I don't remember who initiated it, but one of us finally called the other to say, "This is really silly. Every time we talk, we do it through the lawyers and pay out more money." So we decided that we would begin to talk and finish up the loose ends ourselves. It wasn't many weeks later that we began to talk and resolve the issues as they arose. Heri said he was to be in San Francisco and asked me to dinner. I said yes, and from then on, we became civil with each other. There was little left between us, but at least we were civil. It was obvious that we enjoyed each other's company despite our differences and finally, at last, the hurt was over.

Heri continued living in Stockton and I lived in Emeryville and occasionally we would get together for dinner or a movie. This continued for two-and-a-half years. I continued to go to work and travel but was so lonely. I asked myself, Why am I doing this? I should go home. I didn't know if I would go home and look for a job, but I knew I needed to have roots in New Mexico. So I began to look for a house. I found that the cost of houses had almost doubled, so I had one built on the west side of Albuquerque, requiring only that it faced south. I was never going to shovel snow again.

I told ETS that I wanted to go home and I retired once again. By the time I got there, my brother-in-law had become very ill. So there was a period of two weeks when I took complete care of him and immersed myself in family. It was a salve on my soul which was sorely needed, but by the end of the first two weeks, I got a call—this time from the Pentagon. Once again, I put my belongings in storage and was off to another adventure.

The Pentagon and I

I thought my family would be shocked when I told them that I was already going to leave retirement behind again to go to work for my country, this time at the Pentagon. They had always appreciated my high level of energy, but I didn't know if they were ready for my taking off once more. I loved my family and I was excited about my new casita, but I truly missed the thrill of fast-paced jobs.

Even though I had only begun my retirement just two short weeks ago, I had already become stir crazy. Yes, I was busy helping with my family, but the element of excitement and exhilaration my life had always held was missing. I constantly caught myself drifting back to my tour of duty in Honduras when my life had been so active. I thrived on just a few hours of sleep each night. The embassy was always buzzing with activity and lots and lots of people. It was well guarded by marines. I admired those young men. I didn't know much about the military or their insignias and occasionally called a corporal "colonel" by mistake. They loved it. They were young and full of life. I felt sorry for them because their lives were so strict and regimented. They would even get in trouble for playing music too loud in their marine house. I tried to incorporate them as much as I could in the activities that were going on in the residence. I had always wished that I didn't have to maintain the formality with them that was required, but I couldn't alter their smart salute every morning when I arrived at work each day.

Every morning, usually before 8:00 A.M., I would eagerly climb the stairs to my office. The stairway was lined with pictures of all the U.S. ambassadors that had served in Honduras. They were all men until you got to my picture at the top. Every time I went up those stairs, I said to myself (after pinching my arm to make sure I wasn't dreaming), "Yeah, here I am."

At the top of the stairs were two offices, one belonging to my deputy chief of mission, and then mine. Once the staff realized that I wasn't going to straggle in late using a party as an excuse, but rather, come in early, they began to do the same. Everyone went to work extra early. They respected my work ethic and endeavored to do the same. I valued my team.

My office was as opulent at the embassy as at the residence, and just as huge. Two grand flags, one being the U.S. flag, and the other being the flag of the ambassador, stood on each end of a heavy, highly polished mahogany desk. The brown leather upholstered chairs and couches were made in the same style, and one could get lost sitting in them. It was beautiful, but not really my taste, because they were too masculine. But I had the same opinion about the offices as I did about the residence. So, instead of spending time and money to redecorate, my secretary and I just brought in plants and flowers that wouldn't quit. It became Mari-Luci's room with very little effort.

I had the chairs situated rather informally so that when the country team consisting of eleven or twelve men came to meet with me every morning, we would feel closer. I didn't hold myself apart from them and we quickly became a smoothly running team. These men headed the divisions represented by the United States in this foreign country. There was the head of the Peace Corps, head of the United States Agency for International Development, head of security, the military, and on and on. We talked about what was new in our work and what we might be able to accomplish. We also looked for ways to help each other across areas of expertise. There was much reporting and we also addressed written proposals.

In the beginning, these reports and proposals could have become something of a problem because these men probably were not used to the ambassadors reading them so carefully. But the word got around fast: "Oh, my God, she reads everything you give her and what's more, she circles typos and writes questions in the margins in red!" But I promptly got my team pulling in one direction. They were all fine professionals and it was easy to do. I would ask for their advice, not knowing at the time that they appreciated my requests. I never told anyone, "I'm being successful." I never told anyone anything about how I did my job. But my team started telling the various Washington offices in the State Department. Pretty soon it came back to me that I was doing it right, thanks to my great team.

I was happy to hear this because I really wondered what the folks back home were thinking. This was partly due to some of the small dinner parties Heri and I held for visitors from Washington. One in particular had me in a dilemma with that darn protocol. Since it was our first occasion to entertain guests from Washington, I had told the staff to be on their best behavior. They always followed my instructions to the letter and this time was no different. During dinner, I had a runny nose that wouldn't quit. I couldn't very well pick up my heavily starched white linen napkin to blow it, and I couldn't wipe it on my sleeve. To make it worse, Emily Post, whose book I was in the throes of reading, says that the hostess must never get up from the table unless the house is on fire. I didn't know what to do and I was desperate.

When one of the waiters went by with some food, I whispered to him, "Please bring me a few squares of toilet paper." I had asked for toilet paper because the bathroom was closer than the tissue box and the object of my despair had almost reached my upper lip. What a mistake! I thought it would be quicker, but the waiter took forever to return. I was almost ready to give up and stand up when the door opened and in he walked carrying a highly polished silver platter with an ironed doily and a roll of toilet tissue on it. Needless to say, Heri and I broke into all kinds of laughter. Because I had told the staff that we needed to go first class for our Washington visitors, they weren't about to bring me just any old square of toilet tissue.

While the government paid for any entertaining expenses when Hondurans were included, they expected us to personally pay for our own food and the entertainment of Americans. These parties tended to be quite expensive and the thought that ambassadors get rich while on their tours of duty just isn't true. In fact, when we went home, we were happy that we hadn't been forced to dig into our savings, but we hadn't been able to put any away, either. One of the biggest compliments I received at the end of my tour was from an individual who worked in the administration offices. He came up to say good-bye and said, "Madame Ambassador, I want you to know I've been in the administration cone [branch] in the foreign service for twenty-seven years and I've never seen a more honest ambassador than you." Honesty has its rewards.

Yes, after only two weeks in Albuquerque, I really missed the positive action of my important work. I wasn't ready to retreat. If I could, I still wanted to help improve the quality of life for people and now I had even more skills and knowledge with which to do so. While I tried to accept retirement, I just wasn't ready. So when I got this latest call from Washington asking if I would help with defense policy for Latin America, I said, "Yes!" At least this time, I didn't respond with "Who, me?"

They told me they weren't looking for someone who necessarily knew military matters—they had enough of those experts—rather, they needed a person that understood the idiosyncrasies of the Latin American world. They knew I could talk with Latinos and get their input related to the policies that we were starting to develop. I could easily make many more friends for our country, and that I loved.

This new directive struck a chord in me. I hadn't heard many statements like "We're going to ask the Latinos what they think." The fact that their opinions might be considered excited me and I was pleased but feeling guilty. The last time, I left my mom and grandma, never to see Nanita again. This time I was leaving a sick brother-in-law and couldn't shake the feeling that this was similar to what I felt when leaving my grandma. I went to tell my sister, this time being able to talk about it right away. Before I even got out all the details, my brother-in-law said, "Go, hermanita, go! It's a fabulous opportunity for you to put your skills to work. You had great fun the last time; I bet this will be more of the same. I'm OK. I'm OK." I knew that he wasn't, but was instead seriously ill and would probably be gone soon. His illness had dampened his high spirits and I could sense it.

That was why I had sought only his blessing, because he was the important one this time. I didn't really consult my children. They were already grown and busy with their own lives and families. They all volunteered that I should accept; I think perhaps they knew I wasn't quite ready for retirement. Here I was, home with all this energy and wanting to always be "on the go." The Pentagon was offering me a new adventure I couldn't refuse.

I pulled out a few pots, pans, and bedclothes from my storage that had been brought to my garage and sent it off; it had never been unpacked. My stuff never saw the inside of my house. Amazingly enough, with all my years of moving, I only lost one box containing Christmas decorations from friends. It was very sad because these things were special to me. But I could not bring them back.

I ran across the street to tell my new neighbor whom I had just met that I was leaving again. She must have thought I was crazy and was not going to be a very good neighbor. I quickly worked out a deal with my daughter and her family to take care of my house while theirs was remodeled to put up for sale. I hoped this would help them make a little more money.

I was feeling tremendously excited. I thought to myself, "Bless you, Lord! Someone wants me even after I've retired!"

Retirement for me had meant the end of my professional life. Since my professional life had been such a central part of my existence, I had debated in my head whether it was a good idea or not to retire, but I also knew I had to come home. But once there, I realized that I wasn't ready to stay home . . . not just yet.

The other thing that enticed me was that I was told that I would help create defense policy. There would be opportunities to travel to Latin America and consult with all the countries so we would have their opinions and contributions in formulating this policy. This really roused my interest. In all the international work I had done, I had never seen, with the exception of a very few people in the State Department, any feeling that Latinos could come to the table and contribute great thoughts and share dynamite experiences as they did. But I knew they could.

I thought about my growth from being just a "shoemaker's daughter" into "not the same little Mexican," and finally an assistant vice president of a gigantic company. While once I was afraid to eat a tortilla in public, now I had spoken as an equal with world leaders. Anyone else who wanted to could do this too with enough education and appropriate experiences.

So after one of the briefest retirements in history, I joined the workforce once again, this time as deputy assistant secretary of defense for Latin America. This new assignment entailed heading an office composed of both civilians and military personnel. They were supposed to be trying to hire equal numbers of both sets. That ideal wasn't quite up to par in my office. It had a few more military personnel than civilians when I arrived. Civilians were mostly career people who worked at staffing the Pentagon for a lifetime. There were a few political appointees in some of the slots because their political party had won.

This was a good combination of civilians that were supposed to be apolitical and very aware of what the president and the administration wanted, a healthy dose of appointees that were not political but who had the expertise, and also some highly political ones. With the mixture of military personnel and civilians, I inherited an instant office and staff. Because they were downsizing everywhere, there were never new slots, but there was always a promise that when people left, one could appoint whomever one chose.

However, it wasn't really that easy. The bureaucracy was very active and very tight. There was a great deal of pressure to hire particular inside people. There was constant movement within the organization of staffers trying to advance in their jobs. In the end, I felt that I had never really created my own team. It was a team that was there. But, because I like people, once more I rolled up my sleeves and got to work with whomever was there.

The State Department and the Pentagon often looked at each other suspiciously. Their boundaries of territory were not crystal clear, so I understood why there was always a constant tug between them. Because of this, the Pentagon asked that I use my influence with my friends across the river. I helped push for a slightly better communication system between the two. We were able to establish joint working groups, which brought our thinking closer together.

My days in that particular office were very interesting. There were still staff meetings in the morning, but they weren't quite as pivotal as the country team's meetings at the embassy. They were more of an informative nature in which each of us could tell what we planned to do for that day, what we had heard, and how we could support each other. What was different here in the Pentagon was that the second in command, my deputy, was a high-ranking military officer. I quickly confirmed that the military was a closely knit group. They would always first look to each other for guidance; even basic eye contact gave them away.

Realizing I would have to work with that as a given, I would need to know what the American military thought about what we were doing at every step of the game. So I befriended some of the military, enabling me to know where the military was leaning. It wasn't to be sneaky, but it was necessary if the civilians were going to have any input at all.

My biggest agenda item was to discuss our developing poli-cy. For so long, we had been the ones that helped one way or another to sustain Latin American dictatorships in their respec-tive countries. Today most of those countries are democracies. Some may be very weak, fledgling democracies, and some exist in name only because they have just had elections. But the majority are trying to create meaningful democracy. Neverthe-less, my thinking and that of others was that we should capital-ize on that phenomenon. The policy we should create would be based on a democratic point of view concerning the military. How the military should operate in a democracy would be our guiding principle. When I arrived, my immediate supervisor was a brilliant diplomat and he encouraged this type of modern, broader thinking.

So throughout the two years I was at the Pentagon, I was constantly traveling back and forth to Latin America. I did so with the objective of convincing the most important people in the military and in the departments of foreign relations to work together for the good of their country. It became my new per-sonal campaign. Many ministries of foreign affairs did not trust the leading military officers of their respective nations because most of them were or had been dictators. There was little trust on the part of the educated civilians who valued democracy. The goal for everyone working on these policies was to promote trust between the two powerful groups.

My personal techniques to help this process along were the same ones I had used as an ambassador. I immediately began to make friends in every country I could, create dialogue, find opportunities for deeper discussion, and get people to talk across self-imposed boundaries. I had an open-door policy and any time any foreign military officer was visiting in Washington, I hoped he would come see me, even though at the Pentagon, that was slightly difficult.

There was little funding in the Pentagon at my level for entertaining. In fact, inside my inherited desk, someone had left a dozen or so tin cups, not stoneware or ceramic, but blue enameled tin. So I bought cups and added to the coffee coffers in order to serve guests. When Latin Americans would invite people to visit their countries, they treated them royally. There appeared to be no awareness of that here and I wanted to reciprocate in kind the "bienvenida," or welcome, I always received in Latin America.

I heard many comments like "Why are so many ambassadors coming? We've never seen so many visit before." It was because I was I inviting them everywhere I went and made them feel welcome. I not only welcomed the military attachés, which was common enough to do, but their bosses, the ambassadors, as well. The more people involved in thinking through policy, the bigger the impact would be. This included the U.S. military, members of foreign militaries, the various embassies, the State Department, and the departments of foreign relations—quite an impressive list.

My immediate boss was very knowledgeable about the world and I enjoyed working with him. He had served as an ambassador and was a State Department employee. He was one of the most brilliant men I have known. He really saw the way our policies had always treated Latinos and how they needed to be adjusted to reflect more modern times. So it was wonderful working with him. There were a few policies that I disagreed with and would have liked to see changed. But that wasn't possible, even with a great boss. There's no way to change policies that you, personally, disagree with if the president feels it's the right policy to have. When he left, I was immediately impressed with his successor. He was brilliant and a hard worker.

I was very comfortable with all the other policies because they respected the views of our military and, to the degree possible, the views of at least some Latin Americans. Secretary Perry was a real advocate of encouraging various military establishments to legitimately support democracy throughout the region. The policy before had been that any popular movement or social upheaval in any country in the hemisphere should immediately be put down by the military because such disturbances were always attributed to communists. Our country refused to see that some of the unrest was perhaps entirely justified. We had supported the dictatorships that were composed of the military and by and large, supported by the wealthy. But back then, we saw communists behind every bush and our policies reflected that view.

President Clinton began to make wonderful overtures to most of the countries in the hemisphere, bringing the regional leaders to a summit in Miami to talk about ways to cooperate and help solve problems. The military institutions were not invited. But they had been playing many of the leading roles in their countries, whether the civilians wanted them to or not. They had to be brought in sometime for important discussions. "No, no, they can't be brought in. Our dialogue should be strictly for civilians," I heard constantly.

We finally found a brilliant solution by finding a venue where we could work across boundaries and bring both the military and Foreign Service professionals into high-level discussions. There was much fear on the part of many civilians, both American and foreign. Many people said, "It isn't a good idea. If you bring military together from the various countries, they'll bond and go home promoting more oppression."

My boss, staff, and I kept arguing, "That's not so. Bring countries together to ponder and discuss how a modern military must act in a democracy. That's very different from the context in which they acted before." Our attitude wasn't one of a Pollyanna; we knew the changes wouldn't happen overnight. It took hundreds of years to get where we were now. But we had to make an effort to start the change soon for them. We should be supporting those who were already in the process.

We started to talk about a ministerial for defense ministers of all the thirty-three countries of the Americas with the exception of Cuba. Let me clarify the term "American" and dispel any misconception there might be as to who Americans are. Americans include people from the entire hemisphere, and this includes everyone living anywhere in North, Central, and South America.

The United States does not hold exclusive rights to the term; although the way we use it gives that impression. That is one of the problems that many Latin Americans have with us. They consider themselves Americans also and many think us vain for seeing ourselves as the only Americans.

We needed to get all these Americans together, and many would be meeting for the first time. But we first had to convince the internal bureaucracy at the Pentagon and the powers within it that this was a good idea. Then we had to convince the State Department. When that was done, it was on to the office of the vice president. Finally, we convinced enough people within the Pentagon, within the State Department, and from selected staff from the vice president's office that it was a good idea. From then on, all were able to move smartly ahead to plan and implement such a meeting. I had never pushed my personal powers of speech and persuasion to the limit as I did for this latest cause, and I often did so one-on-one whenever I could. Every drop of experience I had gained from childhood to ambassador to vice president of ETS and on and on was called upon. This had been one of my toughest but perhaps greatest accomplishments.

The summit was held in July of 1995 in Williamsburg, Virginia, the place where our democracy started. Every brick there is permeated with history. A stroll down any of the lanes was a stroll with great men that helped form our democracy such as Thomas Jefferson, George Washington, Patrick Henry, George Mason, and many more. What a beautiful message was brought forth without saying a word.

We had to visit most of the countries personally to convince each minister to attend with their foreign affairs personnel. We knew that some countries would be quite upset about such a meeting for many different reasons. For example, one country did not have a unified leadership. It had separate heads for the navy, air force, and army, and they wouldn't necessarily want only one person to attend. They also wouldn't want to come if the United States was going to tell them how their military should be organized. Two countries [Peru and Ecuador] were engaged in a war; maybe they'd come, and maybe they wouldn't. Much depended on their perceptions of which side in the conflict they thought the United States had taken. These were all legitimate concerns, and we needed to quiet such fears.

I visited some of these countries while my boss and staff went to others. I visited the first and what we considered to be the most strategic country to convince to attend. We believed that if this country wouldn't come, many others might not either. It could start a precedent.

During our preparations, I was counseled to speak only English at this upcoming meeting. This was difficult for me to do because when I was in Latin America, I had always spoken Spanish everywhere I went. But I assumed that the counselors preparing me for these meetings knew what was best, so I kept reminding myself, "Don't speak in Spanish—English only, English only."

By the time I arrived and my contingency and I were on one side of the table and their military and foreign affairs office representatives were facing us from the other side, I thought I was ready. I opened the meeting and told them why we were there, explaining that we were interested in having a ministerial. Because their situation was different from that of some of the other countries, we felt we should approach them first for their thoughts on making this ministerial work.

I had barely gotten started in my prolific English, when all of a sudden, the man seated directly across from me raised his hand for me to stop speaking and said, "Just a minute."

I thought, "Oh, my God. I've already said something that has offended them." They huddled and talked to each other really fast. I wasn't able to understand a word because they were whispering and I began to imagine that it was over before it had begun.

They returned to their chairs and the chairperson looked at me and said, "There's been a request from the people here to ask if you would be willing to speak in Spanish. They're missing a lot when you speak in English."

I relaxed internally and said with much energy and personal pride that once again, my first language was substantiated, "Con todo gusto," I would be delighted to. The discussion followed without a hitch. I had done my homework and it worked. They joined us enthusiastically. From then on, almost every country in the hemisphere was visited and personally invited, all with complete success.

When all the representatives arrived in Williamsburg, it was a sight to see. The commotion their arrival caused was flawlessly handled by the military, which is known for its detailed preparations. The opening ceremony was held at a hotel called The Inn. The room used was richly adorned and had been lined with thirty-three flags, one from each country. What a perfect beginning. Of course, I couldn't hold back my tears from the pride I felt in my country. This ministerial, to me, had completely validated my life. All my struggles as a child were suddenly not important anymore. Not here, not now when the entire western hemisphere could be brought together to talk about policies that would help better all our peoples. Secretary of Defense Perry was at his best. He was a master at getting everybody to speak and everybody got an opportunity. Each and every country was showcased.

All of Williamsburg was utilized. The incredibly beautiful Georgian mansion of Governor Spotswood, the first Governor of Virginia, was used for a dinner and reception. There were big white tents set up in the formal gardens.

With all thirty-three countries represented, there were more than 300 people there. Spanish-speaking male and female U.S. military personnel were assigned to escort each minister, and processions were led by regiments of individuals dressed in colonial style military uniforms. These were navy blue with red lapels and buff-colored trousers. Their eighteenth-century black-powder rifles sported bayonets on the end of the barrels and the occasional sunray that bounced off them reminded me of my first ceremony in Honduras.

The results of this magnificent and historical summit were monumental. The ministers agreed to meet occasionally and start talking about specific problems and ways to correct them. They agreed that it was a good idea to review the role of the military in democracies and begin to see where they might need changes. Some felt that no changes needed to be made, but that was OK too. Countries were looked at one by one. Just bringing everybody together to talk about their needs was a great idea. It had been a remarkable success.

I left the Pentagon right after the ministerial. My friends asked, "Why are you leaving?" For the role my boss and I played in succeeding to bring about the ministerial we both received the Medal for Distinguished Public Service. It is the highest honor a U.S. civilian can receive. Secretary Perry held a wonderful reception in our honor.

He had become more than a superior to me. Even though during the two years I was in the Pentagon I traveled back and forth between countries meeting with defense ministers, ambassadors, and many other high-level people, none of these adventures was as dear to me as traveling with Secretary and Mrs. Perry in their private plane to Honduras, Argentina, and Brazil. Secretary Perry visited these nations for diplomatic reasons and asked my opinions on a variety of matters. I got to give a lot of input into what he would say when he talked with these Latinos. It was a personal triumph for me when he visited Latin America. Since most of his work had been centralized in Europe, everybody speculated that he would never go there. I kept insisting, "Yes, he will. He really cares about the whole world and sees the importance of going there."

At the time, his daughter and son-in-law were on a separate trip in Argentina. I was invited to their private function one night when he and Mrs. Perry went to eat with their children. I was in complete awe at the idea of being able to share their family time.

Their family was much like mine in the exceptional fondness they held for each other. The evening was filled with teasing and laughter and lots of jokes. It was obvious to me that Secretary Perry was the center of this family much the same as my father was with mine. But Secretary Perry held that position with a natural soft-spoken nature and while he made his opinion known, it didn't seem as though he forced it on his family.

Another trip that was memorable was going with Vice President and Mrs. Gore to Latin America in their airplane, Air Force Two. That alone was a unique experience. I had flown in helicopters, small jets, prop planes, and a hydroplane that landed in water, but never in a plane quite like that one.

We flew to Bolivia for serious business talks, but the president of Bolivia and Vice President Gore were school chums and that made it a little more fun. I didn't participate in any of the public ceremonies that were held. I was just a member of the staff, watching and helping when I could.

From there we flew to Argentina. I did participate there with the vice president when he presented congratulations to the Blue Helmets who had just returned from serving the United Nations in Bosnia. We went through the line shaking hands. The first person in line wasn't a Blue Helmet but the wife of one with her two children. Her husband would never return home. I saw a side of Vice President Gore I had never seen on TV. He counseled that lady so beautifully. Placing his hand on the children's' heads in an endearing manner, he said something to the children about their departed dad. "He is not just a hero to Argentina but to the world over," he said without crying.

Not me, though. I kept thinking, Don't listen, don't listen. I knew I was going to cry and my thoughts didn't do a thing to prevent the tears from coming.

The last stop on our trip was Brazil, where the vice president addressed an environmental conference. This conference was very important for environmentalists the world over and I was happy to see that he had come, his presence making a statement in itself.

Despite the honor bestowed on me by Secretary Perry on behalf of the United States, I had a funny feeling about lingering any longer in Washington. I had just performed well in my job and was on such a high that I was able to hide the fact that I was in terrible pain. By the last year I was there, I was in pain all the time. Sometimes I would close my office door for a few minutes just to deal with it, then open the door and go on. It was a tough time.

The pain I felt was due to a serious problem I had endured throughout my entire adult life. I had cysts in my breasts and toward the end of my tour at the Pentagon, my doctor was aspirating them almost weekly. The condition worsened to the point where he suggested that I perhaps should consider a radical operation. I panicked! I didn't like doctors, hospitals, or anything to do with medicine. It was very hard for me to consider, especially since I had few close friends in the area to talk to and I didn't want to call my family and get them worried. So I continued to keep it to myself, feeling disconnected to everything.

The final event that made me decide to go home occurred while I was at the Pentagon. I walked everywhere fast in my high heels, not wanting to waste even a minute, just as I had done my entire life. Somehow, I had never learned to walk slowly and in a more "ladylike" way. One morning, I took a very fast corner toward the ladies' restroom. Somebody had spilled water on the floor and I skidded, hitting the floor with my elbow. My arm hurt instantly. My palm hurt also and I thought the injury was due to that. I got up, washed my hands, checked to see if I had ripped my hose, and made sure my hair wasn't messed up and that I still looked professional. I went back to the office and told no one. Toward the end of the day, after my palm had turned dark purple, I did finally tell my secretary.

Well, the conclusion was that it was a really bad bang, but nothing more. I undress in the dark because I sleep with my shades up, so when I went to bed I didn't get a good look at my arm. So the next day, when I went to take my bath where it was light, I saw that my whole arm was purple. It was then that I knew my elbow was broken. I had spent the whole day and night in great pain with a broken elbow.

I called my secretary and told her. I drove myself to the Pentagon where there is a big infirmary. This is necessary because the Pentagon is twice the size of Las Vegas, with approximately 25,000 people and heart attacks occur there quite often. They immediately sent me to a specialist; and after taking X-rays, they pronounced my elbow broken. The treatment was a sling, pain medicine, and therapy, starting right away.

This dilemma presented a serious problem for me. I'm very right-handed. My left hand went to school but didn't learn a darn thing. I couldn't do anything. Living all alone, I began to get a feeling of nostalgia. It got so bad that I began to crave New Mexican foods. One night I was so desperate to eat some salsa but I couldn't open the jar. Frustrated to no end, I took drastic measures. I traveled down the entire sixteen floors from my apartment to seek help in the lobby. There was no one at the desk, so I waited until the first person came by. It happened to be a man who obviously was not in any humor to help an incapacitated woman. I didn't care, though, and asked, "You can see that I have a problem with my arm and this Mexican is dying to eat some salsa. Would you please open this jar for me?"

The man put down his briefcase and opened the jar, but was not very pleasant about it. I felt just terrible. I'm not used to asking people for help. I have always been very independent. I wondered if I should have asked for help, but I pondered that thought for only a moment because my stomach answered for me with a grumbled "Yes." So back up the sixteen flights of steps I went to eat the entire jarful in one sitting.

I was in a sling for two months. I would put on my clothes as best I could and go to work and ask whoever happened to be in the bathroom to button up my blouse if it was in the back or maybe do something with my hair. I couldn't wear earrings for those long two months and felt as if I was not completely dressed.

I did take comfort, though, by color coordinating my slings with the beautiful clothes I had. Every day I got a compliment. One day I might have a royal blue suit and wear a fuchsia and royal blue sling. I had a black one with big white-and-pink polka dots and everyone thought that one quite cheerful. It was still a very difficult time for me even with all the encouragement from my co-workers because I started to realize that I was all alone with a broken elbow and that I had nobody to rely on.

I was vulnerable and very lonely. I wanted to go home to see if I still had any friends. I wanted to hear mariachi music and eat green chile. I wanted to see the beautiful sunsets only New Mexico can produce and the huge moon that hangs on invisible threads in the star-studded sky. So when my daughter Carla asked me if I wanted to rent my house because they had bought one and planned to move out of mine, I said no. I was going home. I wanted to live with the feeling that I was in a brand new house that was all mine. I didn't have to go home and stay with anyone this time. I was going home, this time, finally to stay.

The Next Zigzag

While I was still very young, I received a lesson in
the value of one's roots. My grandparents began
building their home in Sapello one section at a time
because that was all they could afford. Early one
spring, a *golondrina,* or in English, a swallow, built a
nest inside the room that was to be their living
room. She had selected a special place as her home
high up near the eaves of the roof. As all of God's
wild creatures do, she had her children that spring,
raising them in the nest she had built in their home.

When fall came, she and her children had all
flown south, and Grandma and Grandpa had by
then, saved enough money to add the windows and
doors to the living room. Grandma removed an
adobe brick near the nest during the construction
so that the following spring the swallow could use
it as an entrance to her nest. All the family, friends
and neighbors laughed at her. They told her the
golondrina would never come into the house once
people were living in it. But Grandma said, "Las
golondrinas siempre vuelven a su nido," meaning in
English "They always return to their nests."

Grandpa never questioned Grandma's desires
and when the winter winds began to blow, he
stuffed rags in the hole to keep out the snow and

cold. The following spring, as part of Grandma's spring-cleaning ritual, she whitewashed all the walls. This year she included the swallow's nest and rather than a mud color, it became white. Everyone waited, making jokes when Grandpa pulled out the rags from the hole that would become the swallow's door.

Sure enough, just as Grandma said she would, the golondrina came back, laying her eggs and raising her children in her whitewashed nest.

Every fall she and her children left and Grandpa plugged up the hole for the winter. Every spring he would again unplug it and Grandma would paint the walls and nest after finding a particular type of soil, creating a different color of paint for her walls to welcome back her boarder. She mixed the soil with water and used a sheepskin to apply it to the adobe. In addition, she would always paint a *sanefa*, a border, of a different color using a piece of wool or potato for this part of her art.

What a wonderful sight to see! We witnessed the whole process of life high up in her living room. That bird was a member of the family and when she and her children would go to bed at night, Grandma made us turn off the kerosene lamp in the living room so we wouldn't keep the *pajaritos* awake. No wonder we children grew up loving birds. We saw a marvelous first-hand example of how one should care for and respect God's creatures. By example, that small golondrina taught us to listen to the inner voice we all have inside that draws us toward home.

I hadn't thought of the golondrina for many years, but after attempting to get around with my arm in a sling and the thought of further health challenges, the voice inside me was practically shouting at me, "¡Regresa a Nuevo México!" I remembered Nanita's golondrina returning so faithfully year after year, until the year she didn't come back and we knew she had died, and after much thought, I once again loaded up my boxes and headed for home, this time to stay! Once and for all, I was going to retire and mean it!

I felt I had contributed enough for one lifetime in the struggle for human rights to deserve my retirement. But because I have always been troubled by the nature of the relationship between the United States and Latin America, I found myself yet again wanting to dive right back into the thick of things. Everywhere one turns there is evidence that people with Latino blood running in their veins could still be victims of untrue stereotypes. "They're not as smart. They don't have the experiences we have. They're lazy. They're unschooled." I still hear these accusations and just can't seem to allow them to pass.

These feelings were strong in me even as a child. Seldom was anything positive or true heard about Mexico in the United States. My own grandmother spent many nights and lots of oatmeal trying to lighten my skin color. She knew that even in Las Vegas, with such a long history of Spanish influence, there was always that undercurrent of "you're not as good as I am."

Our countrymen have created an artificial border to separate Mexico and the United States. At the same time, our government has mostly looked to Europe for solutions. Not without ridicule, we have finally participated in the creation of NAFTA, but not before we turned toward Asia as our best market. When will the United States see the wealth that exists in Latin America, both in terms of human resources and the economy? If the Latin Americans were to seek other business partners, we would get very upset, but we are pushing them in that direction.

We see ourselves as a beacon of light for the whole world, but continue to live in darkness concerning our own next-door neighbors. Many citizens of the United States don't realize that the problems of Latin America are our problems as well. Citizens and politicians alike continue to put them on the "isolated side of the playground."

After working all over the world to help in my small way to join all peoples in equality, I reflect back to when I was in high school. We were given tests to see what we were going to be when we grew up. Back then, I had no idea what my life had in store for me. I remember not wanting even to take a test to see what I was talented at, because I knew what I wanted to be. I told everyone, teachers included, that I wanted to be a court reporter in Latin America. Where that dream came from, I have no idea. I didn't type and didn't know what a court reporter did except for a movie I had seen once. But I wanted to be in Latin America because I was very proud that I spoke "beautiful Spanish." I saw myself doing something very exotic.

I used to tell my mom that I would love to do some kind of secretarial work in Latin America. She was so sweet. She never told me that I was a very poor typist and didn't do things very well with my hands, but it stayed in me and when the opportunities came to work in Latin America, I couldn't believe my luck. The reporter part never came in. But I was in and out of every institution you can imagine in just about every country in Latin America over and over.

When I was named United States ambassador, I recall Mom telling me, "Sweetheart, your dream of going to live in Latin America has been fulfilled." It touched me that my mother who, despite her lack of education and experience further than her small hometown, remembered after all those years what I wanted to be when I grew up.

So now, even with my final retirement, I still can't seem to stop confronting such a disparity felt by the Latinos. It motivates me and I have found that I haven't lost one drop of energy. There's just no way I can sit still allowing any injustice when I might be able to make a difference, even if it's a small one.

Never able to leave the struggle for human rights, I have joined boards that can make a difference in the lives of the poor. I hold office in the AgriFuture Foundation Board. The Foundation was created by the International Institute for Cooperation in Agriculture (IICA). All thirty-three countries in the hemisphere are active participants. While the Foundation is just a fledgling institution, there's great potential for helping the poorest of the poor in the hemisphere. One of those places is Haiti.

A project was started there with the poorest women in a rural area. They were given bank loans to help them buy seed. They are the growers of the vegetables for their families. We tried to get them to improve the quality of their vegetables and find ways to barter with each other.

The first year was a great success. All the women paid the entire loan back during the year with the exception of one who passed away. Her loan was paid in full by all the other women. These people have demonstrated a spirit of survival, honor, and dignity. What a great first year! This year, the women have asked for a donkey to take some of their produce to market. It seems they are growing a few extra vegetables and would like to sell them. We are anxiously waiting to see their success.

I also joined a national commission sponsored by the College Board in New York that is searching to help gifted Hispanic youth. Because so much energy is spent bringing in those who are left out, a group of very gifted youngsters coming from families that don't necessarily have as many financial difficulties has been ignored. We are studying what might be done about encouraging and assisting those talented young people.

It was a different direction for me; I had always worked to reach the poorest of the poor. But I was convinced after seeing the facts that this void is something we need to address in a serious way.

Recently I joined the Hispanic Culture Foundation and currently serve as secretary. It is the fund-raising arm of the National Hispanic Cultural Center. The center was established to identify, promote, enhance, and preserve the Hispanic culture through the arts and humanities. This is a viable idea close to my heart, and the center is even located in Albuquerque, my home town.

My life is still moving at a fast clip. I travel to at least one foreign country a year but sometimes I am able to visit several. A great joy was last year (2000) when I was the house guest of Ambassador Frank Almaguer and his wife in Tegucigulpa, Honduras. I relived my days as an ambassador and saw many wonderful friends. That was a real highlight of my constant globetrotting.

I do not know that I will become a home-body anytime soon. It is not in my bones. I tend to a large number of houseplants and do all my own gardening during the days I do spend at home. I also spend hours and hours rearranging my furniture and artifacts, just as my mother taught me to do so long ago. Decorating is in my blood.

I still pray often, both for myself and for all my friends who ask me to pray for them. I often attend services throughout the week and sometimes twice on weekends. The Most Holy Rosary Church has provided me with a real spiritual home. I was elected a member of the parish pastoral council, which is an honor that I accepted humbly.

My children and grandchildren, with the exception of one grandson, live in New Mexico. I visit them several times throughout the year. I even get to take one grandson to his weekly tuba lessons. That is a weekly blessing I can count on, as are my visits with my sister. In addition, my granddaughter and I spend one week together all by ourselves.

Mi familia.

I know that I am still the daughter of a bugler in Pancho Villa's army who had a dream. And, I hold dear all the teachings my family passed on to me. Those people gave me the gift of who I am. But I also realize that I have grown beyond my simple beginnings. While my shyness is right under the surface, I have engaged in many campaigns for those who can't speak out for themselves against poverty, abuse of human rights, and racism.

My life has been one of many, many marvelous surprises. The greatest of these has been the many turns in the road my life has taken. Growing up in an impoverished home, in a poor community where higher education was not necessarily valued or aspired to by many people, this timid one got through. As I reflect on my life, I know there are many adventures still to come.

What they will be, I don't know, but I'll see you at the next zigzag. Hasta luego.